This Is What I'm Saying

Burdens of a Midwestern Suburban Polymath

Scott Robinson

ISBN 978-1548227999

Author photograph by Joshua Robinson

For my friend David Burt,

whose voice greatly improved my hearing

Also by Scott Robinson ...

The Beatles Guide to Love & Sex

To the Toppermost of the Poppermost:

Exploring the #1 Hits of the Beatles

Living Like Beatles

Rock Candy: The Beatles

The Quotable Beatles

LP: The Beatles

LP: Celebrating the Lost Art of Album-Oriented Rock

Ten Perfect Years: Rock Music's Cambrian Explosion, 1966-1975

Sing For the Years: Exploring the Greatest Songs of Classic Rock

YesTales: An Unauthorized Biography of Rock's Most Cosmic Band

Red Brains, Blue Brains: Neuroscience and Donald Trump

Red Brains, Blue Brains: Authoritarian We Will Go!

The Paleo Guide to Leadership and Team Building

The Paleo Guide to Human Resources

Lucy's Courtship: The Role of the Feminine in Human Evolution

Chasing the Enterprise:

Achieving *Star Trek*'s Vision of the Human Future

Infinite Diversity in Infinite Combination

Uncle Scott's Treasury of Useless Knowledge

Uncle Scott's Treasury of Random Information

My Work Here is Done!

More Very Random Essays on Weighty Matters

Shadows of Shadows

Table of Contents

Acknowledgments

A number of the ideas presented in the observations that follow derive from years of dialog, debate and research with Dr. Jerald Hughes of the University of Texas - Rio Grande Valley. My gratitude for our long intellectual partnership and endless array of shared interests can never be sufficiently expressed.

I'm also deeply grateful for the private Facebook community to which we both belong, Fixing the World – a community of thoughtful, gracious minds who inspire me daily.

Finally, I submit this collection in remembrance of the first polymath I ever knew – John Henry Emrich, my maternal grandfather, whose quiet interests ranged from physics to astronomy to woodworking to Agatha Christie, with hefty doses of Asimov thrown in. He always brought a book for me when he visited, which set the course of my life.

Introduction

The minds we admire most are minds that roam freely. From Isaac Asimov to Thomas Jefferson, from Ada Lovelace to da Vinci to Steve Jobs, the author is a huge fan of people who think and feel across a broad spectrum.

This collection of tidbits is in that tradition – letting the mind bounce from here to there, embracing interesting ideas along the way and seeing where they lead. Many of the ideas that follow received thoughtful and insightful review and deliberation in discussion with friends and colleagues online, and hopefully some sense of that community comes through: few things are as pleasurable as the consideration of intriguing concepts by curious minds.

The themes here summarize a lengthy season of attention to several important topics: human cognition, its deep history and social dysfunctions; empathy; politics and religion; economics; anthropology and, of course, bonobos.

No hold on truth is claimed, and the author's limitations in perspective and worldview are, in fact, of a piece with the thematic thread presented. Lest the whole exercise seem pretentious (it was born on the Internet, so that's to some degree inevitable), be assured he will be perfectly happy if the only result is that these recent thoughts lead the reader to new ones.

The Curse of the Like-Minded

"The sound of tireless voices is the price we pay for the right to hear the music of our own opinions."

~Adlai E. Stevenson

Like-mindedness is something we consider a virtue by default. When we are surrounded by others who think and feel as we do, we experience great social comfort and safety.

And it is true that there are many social contexts in which like-mindedness is a plus - elective activities that provide enjoyment and bonding, like sports preferences. But when it comes to guiding a society and making decisions affecting everyone, like-mindedness becomes a toxin.

Human beings live in groups too large to manage. Our brains are insufficient to provide the empathy and understanding and cooperation that we enjoyed earlier in human history within groups of tens of thousands and millions, and this is ultimately the source of the violence and rage and brokenness we experience in the modern world. A consequence of our out-sized groups is that it is possible for people who think one way to congregate into sub-groups, which is unhealthy to both the individual and the group.

And in consequence, we have war, racism, inequality, and other hideous abuses. At the root of each is like-mindedness.

Human beings function best when many minds join together in community, unafraid to confront and even enjoy the differences. But this can only happen when we realize the value of other minds and recognize/resist our own default impulse to sequester away with those who reflect our own thoughts. We need to quell that impulse, when we can, and cultivate a new one --- a hunger to experience and understand minds not like our own.

On the Basis of Empathy

"When you look in his eyes, you know that somebody's in there..."
~"Old Folkie," Harry Chapin

Human beings are unique among the creatures of earth for many reasons, and the greatest of these is not our use of language or our bipedalism, but our social organization. There are many creatures that form groups, and some thereby capable of complex behaviors, but none capable of combining such refined individualism with such variable group coordination.

Unique, but just barely: our two immediate cousins, the chimpanzee and the bonobo - who are genetically equidistant from us - also demonstrate very complex social order combined with great individual variety. We three species were one, 8 million years ago, but when we came out of the trees and learned to walk, our cortical development accelerated, and here we are. The traces of our pre-divergent ancestor remain, however, and a close look at our cousins is informative of who we are inside, and our potential yet untapped.

The chimpanzee is aggressive, warlike, patriarchal and socially oriented around dominance. Superficial surveys of ape anthropology draw comparisons between the chimpanzee and us, and conclude that this reflects our common ancestor and thus seals our fate.

But over the past 50 years, study after study has overturned this notion: there is no substantive evidence, across the past three million years, that the various brands of hominid immediately preceding ourselves behaved as chimpanzees do, even though many of us do today.

The bonobo, on the other hand, is comparatively peaceful, far more cooperative, and more socially integrated than the chimpanzee - and, in many ways, ourselves. Bonobo society is not fully egalitarian, but what hierarchy exists is based on seniority, not physical aggression, and is shared between the genders - males do not dominate[1].

---

[1] See *Sex At Dawn* (2010), by Christopher Ryan and CacildaJethá for an excellent elaboration of these distinctions.

In short, the bonobo displays far more empathy - equal to ourselves in potential, superior to us in day-to-day living.

What is the difference? And why are we, the most developed of the three, in limbo when it comes to empathy?

The difference is this: chimpanzees track the head movements of other chimpanzees; bonobos look into each other's eyes.

And so do we. Gazing into the eyes of one's own kind is the window into the development of the conscious self.

There's a lot more going on here, to do with sexual behaviors and brain organization, but in a nutshell, the human capacity for empathy is through the roof: what limitations we observe today, we brought on ourselves, by going a little chimpanzee when we learned to harvest energy. We had it good there, for hundreds of thousands of years; we can have it that good again...

(Turn to Page 35)

Human Community is Broken

It is a cornerstone of emerging social theory that most of human social history (300,000 YA - 12,000 YA) occurred in a very different social universe than the one we've engineered since the advent of agriculture. Nomadic human communities in prehistory had very different patterns of social interaction - and those patterns were far more consistent with our cognitive social abilities.

Put another way, we have built a social universe, in ignorance, around the acquisition and control of energy, and consequentially, competition with and control of other human beings - as opposed to the deep cooperation that saw us thru ice ages and constant predation.

This weekend, I spoke of this with someone who, like me, is cognitively distinct. I am an ADD adult (and was an ADHD child), and was having this conversation with someone who has a similar genetically-linked cognitive difference. There are many such differences - ADD, autism, Asperger's, bipolarity - and each is considered, within the context of our Western social frame, a 'disorder.'

Thom Hartmann has spent 20 years making the case that the 'disorder' is not with the people, but with the society around them; he argues that each of these 'disorders' is a naturally-occurring cognitive variation that serves an evolutionary social function.

In the case of ADD, it's an easy argument. Hartmann calls the ADD individual a "hunter child" - a natural pattern-finder, a person whose attention is sharply tuned to environmental variations. In the modern world, where hunting isn't necessary for survival, that attention quirk manifests as artistry and creativity. In other words, eliminate ADD and you eliminate most art and creativity.

And so it is, across the cognitive spectrum: each of the social cognition 'disorders' for which we reject and marginalize others is in fact a set of social features once useful in ways we no longer clearly perceive.

As an ADHD child, and later an ADD adult, I've experienced more than my share of that rejection and marginalization - but I prize the cognitive features that set me apart. And in my weekend conversation, I made the point that it is our society that is dysfunctional - not me, not you, not our children.

In the broader arena, I've had to defend Hartmann's assertion (many others have made it, as well) that we live in a broken social universe. It's an easy case to make.

Off the top of my head - and anecdotally - I am a fan of a period drama on television that takes place in 16th century France. Though it is soundtracked and cast for a young audience, I find it fascinating for its historical authenticity - it follows the actual timeline, framed in the real religious and political tensions of the era. And on this TV show, two vast social groups are in deadly conflict: each group worships and prays to the same transcontinental deity, but one group embraces a social hierarchy by which the deity is addressed, while the other does not. Based on this behavioral distinction, slaughter ensues and blood runs freely, even within neighborhoods.

Moreover, young females of reproductive potential are socially constrained not only in their sexual behavior, but in their freedom to speak or not speak to others, under penalty of social estrangement. Loss of virginity or reputation for modesty means poverty or worse.

Four centuries and an Enlightenment later, we would expect these behaviors to have relaxed considerably - yet today, in the most advanced nation on earth, a deity-focused group has taken political power and is seeking to enforce its own patriarchal paradigm for sexual behaviors, along with male-dominated restriction of female choices - and the disenfranchisement of those not in the same religious group, with outright removal of those in competing religions (who, it must be pointed out, nevertheless worship the same deity).

Do we really want to argue that it is our cognitive outliers, rather than our society, that are hosting the disorder?

We know that these variations in social cognition are all genetically linked - and each is distinguished by behaviors that extract the individual from the expectations of society. The genes are ancient, the expectations very recent. They are by no means universal, and change over time. The labeling and rejection of those born to roll differently aren't simply disingenuous - it is a diminishing of our communities, of our society. Human community flourishes when its every member is cherished.

Scanners

Within each of us, there's an axis of social thought and behavior that derives from our innate feelings about risk. At one end of that axis, there's an extreme aversion to take risks; at the other, an extreme propensity to ignore risk in favor of the pursuit of opportunity.

Most of us fall somewhere between those two extremes: on the one hand, we'll feel uncomfortable playing in the street; on the other, we'll brave the hazards of traffic to go to the grocery store.

Our personal neurology places us wherever on this axis we happen to live. The main driver is the size of our right amygdala lobe, which determines the intensity of our response to threats. Some of us have a lot of tissue in that lobe; some, not so much. It's a roll of the genetic dice: some of us are born to scan for Threat, some are born to scan for Opportunity.

It's not all about the genes, of course; our social training has a lot to do with the behavior that arises from our Threat-scanning/Opportunity-scanning predispositions. But the brain we're born with sets the potential for whatever behaviors emerge.

All this scanning makes its way into our sociopolitical selves. How strongly we reach to outsiders, how focused we are (or are not) on security, and how willing we are to extend public support for people we don't know all derive from this feature of our brains. When we scan for threat or opportunity and score a hit, our brain feels satisfied – it represents a job well done.

The trick is to not hold it against those whose brains don't respond as ours do.

(Turn to Page 32)

Strange Loops

Douglas Hofstadter was once a boy genius. Not long out of graduate school, he won the Pulitzer Prize for his masterpiece *Gödel, Escher, Bach: An Eternal Golden Braid*, a brilliant exposition of concepts and insights and artistic ruminations on the nature of art and mind, real and artificial.

Among these insights was the concept of the Strange Loop, the idea of cyclic structures that move through a system, only to wind up where they started. Kurt Gödel pioneered the idea in mathematics; M. C. Escher, in art; and Johann Sebastian Bach, in music.Hofstadter brought the idea into computer science and explorations of cognition: strange loops, he posited, reside in human minds.

Fast-forward several years. Hofstadter meets and marries Carol Brush; he loves her deeply, and she him, and in the eighth year of their marriage, after they have created a son and a daughter, Carol dies suddenly on holiday in Italy.

For the next 20 years, Hofstadter – grieving continuously, unable to move beyond her death – continues to write and think and theorize around the loss of the love of his life, his true partner.

Then it dawns on him: he himself is a series of strange loops, a recursive, self-referential system whirling endlessly around itself; and he has another insight, a game-changing one – Carol is a strange loop, intermingling with his loops. And this, he realizes, is the true nature of human consciousness.

With the concept of strange loops, and his extended longing for his missing love, Hofstadter happened upon an insight that furthers our understanding of consciousness: each of us is a collection of strange loops, important and persistent pieces of the thoughts and essence of those we love. *Each human being is the sum total of the other human beings who loved them.*

How accurate is this? We aren't yet able to measure it. But it's an insight that resonates deeply: who among us doesn't echo the melodies we discovered in the love of those we cherished?

Sociopolitical Blind Spots

We all see social and political blind spots in others - our crazy Uncle Ralph at Thanksgiving, spouting Tea Party this and that; our wacko cousin Rudy with his conspiracy theories, and so on - but by definition we are insensitive to our own.

The reasons for this insensitivity are rooted in neurophysiology, genetics, and paleoanthropology - a kind of collective primer of human social predisposition to clearly defined perceptions and responses. Contemporary politics and social bias fall into that very broad category.

We are curious about certain groups that can't seem to see the train coming until it runs them over. And, of course, we can see (in hindsight) that we, too, have a shared blind spot, which presents itself when we get hit by events and didn't see it coming.

Certain social preferences indicate natural predispositions that make clear an individual's political point of view - and, by extension, the areas they probably cannot see or understand very clearly. None of us is exempt: because we have perpetual exposure to the real-world exemplars and use cases of the theory, we tend to be emotionally detached in the area of Threat - which means some things sneak up on us.

The point: we *all* have these sociopolitical blind spots, things about other people and groups that we think we understand, but really don't. It's not possible to *not* have them.

"As brainy social animals, human beings evolved to be consummate actors whose survival and ability to reproduce depend on the quality of our performances. We enter the world prepared to perform roles and manage the impressions of others, with the ultimate evolutionary aim of getting along and getting ahead in the social groups that define who we are."

~Dan P. McAdams

On Cynicism

As I write a daily report on the Trump administration's activities - including public reaction - it is hard not to be overwhelmed, if not outright depressed, by the pervasive cloud of cynicism that underlies the dread and uncertainty in everyone engaged in the nation's sudden shifts.

And I think it's more useful to look there, beneath the noise, in search of what needs fixing.

Cynicism, as we conceive it, is not a part of human nature. Negative default assumptions about the nature of others had no place in Paleolithic culture; group survival required egalitarian distribution and a commitment to the well-being of every clan member. There was no place or use for subterfuge, and one's self-interest and group interest were deeply intertwined.

We invented cynicism, in other words. It does not come naturally to us.

We also invented the world that made it possible. We have created layer upon layer of "fake" society and culture, narratives that have nothing substantial to do with our connection to one another or our ultimate well-being as a species; ideology, phone apps and Netflix ultimately provide nothing of value to the tribe.

It is easy to look at the new leader of the free world - a man whose pursuit of self-interest is not only overt but legendary by design, a man so unequipped, so unqualified for his post and so insecure that we have no frame of reference for response - and feel that cynicism is not only appropriate but essential.

It is easy to look at the society that enabled his rise - an America far from its moorings, decades afloat in a sea of middle class exploitation, government by lobby and bankster plunder - and believe that this is the natural order of things.

But I don't believe it. We are unmoored and adrift, yes, but human nature itself has not changed. The man in the Oval Office, however out of place, behaves as he does for the same reasons our distant ancestors did - to survive. We excuse our inner rage and posture as we do, all for the same reason - to survive. We simply need to do a reality check on what that word now means.

It's easy to be cynical. It's harder to push thru the dark cloud and seek out the inner truth of the human experience, far removed from it as we've become - that our fear and dread and insecurity are not the sum of who we are, and that those around us ultimately want and need exactly the same things we do, underneath the layers of social artifice.

We have each other. And when we learn to see one another in the light of prehistory and natural order, there is no inequality in that.

(Turn to Page 39)

(Turn to Page 39)

The GOP Today: Dat Ol' Time Religion[2]

Every Sunday morning, they gather together, singing and chatting and sitting and listening and agreeing. Every Sunday, they huddle in the shelter of their agreement, secure in their momentary collective purity of viewpoint. Surrounded by Us. Isolated from Them. And almost paradoxically, in their homogeneity, they publicly declare, "There is room for all!"

And all is well – until some Big Decision pops up: should we buy a new organ? Should we build a new building? Should we expand our staff? Within weeks, competing ways of deciding begin to clash, as the need to decide draws out and emphasizes differences in styles of thought within the congregants.

A forceful personality emerges on one side or the other, and begins to rally those who think as he does: factions emerge, and those on the wrong side of the divide are declared "not *true* Christians!" by the forceful personality. Taking umbrage – and who wouldn't? – those so labeled respond in kind. Painfully, with much personal harm done all around, a split occurs. People turn away from each other. Life-long friendships end. Where once there stood one church, there now stand two.

Why is he telling us this?

I told you that story so that I could tell you this one …

Back in the Age of Black and White that conservatives think back upon with such longing, they were in fact as factionalized as it is possible to be, recalls George Lakoff of UC Berkeley. There were libertarian conservatives, social conservatives, financial conservatives, militant conservatives, religious conservatives. The social conservatives were not particularly religious, and didn't like the religious conservatives; the social conservatives and the religious conservatives were despised by the libertarians, and by the financial conservatives even more so. The militant conservatives could abide only the libertarian conservatives.

---

[2] Originally published in the blog "That Turns Out Not to Be the Case," August 12, 2012

As Vietnam began to warm up along with color TV, dissipating the Black and White, it dawned on somebody somewhere that all this factionalizing wouldn't get conservatism anywhere. A summit rallied the leaderships of all factions around William F. Buckley, for the purpose of finding common ground and parsing the agree-to-disagree issues. "There is room for all!" they decided, and they all got behind Barry Goldwater for president.

Too little too late, but they rallied again, this time taking note that in the now-blazing glow of Vietnam, young people weren't joining the conservative cause in any great numbers. As Nixon ascended, the Powell Memo emerged[3], offering the conservative leadership a blueprint for harvesting young blood for the party, pulling kids away from their guitars and flowers and morphing them into Alex P. Keaton. Lewis Powell (whom Nixon went on to appoint to the Supreme Court) advocated a deep investment in conservative institutes and think tanks, for the purpose of broad indoctrination. Room for all!

And it worked. Powell's successor, William Simon, Sr., proceeded to arrange the financing of the Heritage Foundation and the Olin Institute at Harvard, and by 1980, the stage was set for Ronald Reagan – and so we have the world we have today.

Along the way, however, the new conservative policy of "Room for all!" had its consequences: the leadership went out of its way to annex the Christian Right, and grabbed hard the tiger's tail, and we all can see how well that turned out for both the GOP and the Evangelical Church. Said Goldwater himself to John Dean in 1994,

"Mark my word, if and when these preachers get control of the [Republican] party, and they're sure trying to do so, it's going to be a terrible damn problem. Frankly, these people frighten me. Politics and governing demand compromise. But these Christians believe they are acting in the name of God, so they can't and won't compromise."

Dr. Jerald Hughes, however, pointed out to me in a recent conversation that the consequences of this union run far deeper:

---

[3]http://reclaimdemocracy.org/corporate_accountability/powell_memo_lewis.html

"We're seeing the basic Protestant Evangelical dynamic at work … They start accusing each other of not being 'true' Christians, and then start scanning for these false Christians, and then become as mean-spirited as possible when they think they've found one. Splits happen. Everyone loses. "It really should have dawned on *somebody*, at Karl Rove's level or at least in his circle, that having loose cannons like Limbaugh running around labeling people RINOs is a way of *shrinking* their party."

Rush Limbaugh becomes the 'forceful personality' who decides who's a 'true' Republican and who's a RINO, and we have every GOP candidate in the nation scrambling and flip-flopping, as needed, to stay on the 'right' side of the divide.

Divide?

Yes, divide. In absorbing the Evangelical Right, the conservative movement has also absorbed the Evangelical DNA, including its tendency to reproduce by fission.

To the casual observer, the conservative compromise of the late-Sixties/early-Seventies may seem intact; putting on a united front is, after all, something conservatives now do skillfully, from long experience. The GOP presents itself as solid and stable, committed to its agenda, all for one and one for all.

Well, that turns out not to be the case.

Within the GOP, unity is all but gone, owing to years and years of Limbaugh, Beck and other talking heads – ham-fisted entertainers with no political experience or intellectual accomplishment of any kind – indulging in their growing power to decide Who Stays and Who Goes.

On the one hand, we have the Neocon faction, old-schoolers in the mold of the fictionalized Reagan: Bush and Cheney, John McCain, Newt Gingrich, Rupert Murdoch, Karl Rove, Mitch McConnell – and, of course, Mitt Romney. On the other hand, we have the Tea Party: Sarah Palin, Rick Santorum, Michele Bachmann, Jim DeMint, Grover Norquist, the Koch Brothers. It's easy to see these two groups as more-or-less the same, when viewed from without: they see themselves as bearers of truth, in the same sense that Evangelicals do; they each leverage themselves by means of the post-Powell Memo conservative infrastructure; and they practice, first and foremost, Identity politics. And they both seem to believe, as Hughes points out, that if they can just get their message across to the masses, the people will finally see the light and scamper into the fold.

But the view from within is very different. Neocons, for all their small-government rhetoric, are fine with big government, as long as it's for-profit (privatized); Tea Partiers want *all* government that isn't the military done away with. Neocons are primarily focused on business, not religion; Tea Partiers want nothing less than a national theocracy. Neocons in political office are about their own political strength; the Tea Party seeks to elect legislators who will work their will, and their will alone.

John Boehner, then Speaker of the House, was forced to straddle this growing divide, watching helplessly as conservative moderates have been relentlessly hunted down and eliminated. The Senate, under Democratic control for the moment, is the only mechanism counter-balancing the Tea Party's agenda.

And it's the Senate where the TP's battle will be fought: they seek not to simply take control back from the Democrats; they seek to eliminate their Neocon cousins in the process. McConnell himself has been targeted, and where Neocon senators can't be replaced, the TP seeks to turn them.

The question now becomes, can this possibly be a winning strategy? Can the church split and still have any hope of holding sway in this sinful world? The GOP reproduction-by-fission we are witnessing today represents the dismantling of decades of careful internal compromise that put the party on the powerful perch it has occupied for more than a generation – compromise that is simply not within the cognitive reach of Evangelical personalities, as Goldwater said all along.

Now that the GOP has taken back the White House and Congress, the nation faces not one but two possible futures. The Neocon vision of the United States and the Tea Party alternative are very different in kind, and both dystopian from the standpoint of those facing systematic disenfranchisement – most of the US population, when one considers that the GOP with both factions only represents 20 percent of us (counting those registered to vote). If the GOP continues to split without some underlying strategy, all the money in the Koch kingdom won't bring the party victory in November. If, on the other hand, the GOP prevails, then the battle to follow will make the current struggle seem like laser tag, as the party hunts down its own, and relegates everyone else to permanent second-class status.

There doesn't seem to be much middle ground, does there? We're counting down to it, and it's going to break one way or another. Just as the nation itself is now very polarized, very black and white, so is the map of the two roads this current split might take. We're either very safe, or very screwed.

Seekers

Just as human brains scan for Threat and Opportunity in naturally randomized ratios, so do they also seek. Specifically, they seek novelty. And Uniformity.

We receive information from the world when something about it seems different – an animal passed this way, or the weather seems to be changing. Our minds use that information to pursue what is good and avoid what is bad.

Similarly, we find it useful when we encounter the familiar – we return to a place we've been before, surround ourselves with others whom we know – and our brains reward us with a feeling of comfort.

As with Threat and Opportunity, an axis of social thought and behavior follows this balance between Novelty and Uniformity. At one extreme is the person who pursues the new and different to the exclusion of all else; at the other is that individual who never leaves the house. And most of us live in between.

This time around, the neurological foundation of the axis is not in brain tissue but in a neurotransmitter – dopamine. It is the "reward" drug in the nervous system, giving us a happy little *ding* every time we've done a good job. Our genes give us some level of receptivity to dopamine: high receptivity means we will be sated more rapidly by a dopamine *ding*; low receptivity means we will get out into the world and grasp for it.

Socially, those with high receptivity tend to cling to the familiar, to eschew change, and to see those with low receptivity as reckless; those with low receptivity tend to see their opposites as overly fearful, or even paranoid.

But, once again, it's all the roll of the genetic dice: Novelty Seekers and Uniformity Seekers all emerge from the same ancient environment. The world needs us all.

(Turn to Page 80)

Cognitive Clusters

A *cognitive cluster* is a social group composed of persons who share the same (or similar) cognitive type - people with the same emotional predispositions about self and others, people of common worldview.

Examples include churches, political parties, activist groups.
Cognitive clusters are extremely common in the social universe we've created, but were not possible in Paleolithic times. When there are only a hundred or so people in your entire social universe, it isn't really possible to segregate by socioeconomic bias. Today, however, populations are so dense that it is no problem at all – it is, in fact, almost too easy.

When we are part of a declustered group - a social circle composed of randomly distributed cognitive types - it is usually by accident, not by choice. Examples include sports teams, school classes, military units.

What are the advantages and disadvantages of these social conditions?

If I'm in a cognitive cluster, I will passively enjoy the following benefits: perpetual validation; very strong group solidarity; high confidence of my group's 'rightness' and problem-solving skills, within a limited domain. These things all make me feel good, so I am likely to firmly commit to the group.

But there are disadvantages as well. While my particular group will reflect my own skill at solving particular kinds of problems, it will be alarmingly lacking at solving problems I am NOT skilled at solving - and there will be little awareness, if not outright denial, of this deficit. Moreover, the sense of 'rightness' driving the group's solidarity will likely lead to 'othering' of those outside the group: they will not be regarded as different, but inferior.

Finally, when I am surrounded by people who see the world as I do, I feel I can outsource my social learning to the group: I don't need to observe others and learn from their behaviors; I can simply accept what my group feels about human behavior, because my group is 'right.'

What about a *de*-clustered group?

If I'm in a group of people of randomized cognitive types, I'm among persons who each view the world differently, view self and others differently, solve problems differently. This cognitive diversity benefits me in a number of ways: this group can, between its members, solve a far greater range of problems together; I will be valued not for my commonality with others, but for my uniqueness; and my group will tend toward inclusion and valuing of those outside the group, who will not be viewed as 'different' than those within the group, since diversity defines the group.

But I will have to work harder to be in this group than I would in a cognitive cluster. I cannot outsource my beliefs to the group, because the group will be host to many beliefs; I cannot outsource social learning to the group, because there will be no one 'right' worldview or behavioral frame - I must keep those skills sharp within myself. And, most importantly, 'right' and 'wrong' will have few defaults; the 'right' thing and the 'wrong' thing will often be matters of group deliberation, in which I will be obliged to participate.

We seldom if ever choose this latter path consciously, though we are often thrust into it by accident. But, like choosing to eat right and exercise daily, it is clearly the healthier choice, despite being harder. Isn't it worth looking at these two courses side-by-side, and choosing consciously, rather than passively?

(Turn to Page 38)

Empathy, continued

Empathy is, in physics metaphor, the strong nuclear force - it binds humanity together, it makes us the creatures that we are. It is the wiring that enables human bonding, the fuel of our unprecedented capacity for cooperation.

Empathy is imperiled, social science now tells us. Western society actively truncates it; empathy is a bane to the economic forces of our era, a human feature that must be carefully throttled in most social frames. Many facets of Western culture carefully cull it, by design.

We in the United States now stand embarrassed before the world, as we are reduced to squabbling schoolchildren throwing mud balls at one another and calling names, as bullies have arisen to taunt us. The Us vs. Them of the post-Goldwater years has now swallowed our discourse entirely, tainted our economy, reversed decades of social progress, and rendered our political process immobile.

The realities of empathy are evident with but a moment of self-reflection: I can look at a sociopolitical opposite at a rally and feel no connection; but when I see the same person struggling on an escalator with three small children, absent any knowledge of their politics, I feel connection in plenty. The conclusion is obvious: we rebel against ideas, but take out our feelings on the messenger.

We *must* push back against Us vs. Them, and I despair even as I t type it, as my liberal/progressive friends, so offended by the behaviors of the Right, saddle up for war; yet I cannot deny that the Democratic Party is by its own hand a victim of the very loss of empathy that drives the growing rage, having lost empathy for those it once defended.

The pushback must include active resistance to bad ideas, hostile words, and destructive policy - but more important than those things is the restoration of empathy. And that need not be political; it can be found in a thousand moments, every day, in every direction. We have but to decide to seek it...
(Turn to Page 46)

Red Brains, Blue Brains

Some brains are red, some brains are blue.

It goes beyond literal differences in brain structure and chemistry: it includes predictors based on emotional responses that are a consequence of those differences (which are not just physical, but genetic).

Both liberalism and conservatism emerge from deep processing that happens in the brain below the level of conscious awareness. There are many reasons we know this to be true, but a very interesting one is our impulsive patterns of attraction/revulsion.

It should go without saying that we can expect a wide range of variability in what individuals find attractive or revolting, and it should go without saying that we do not "choose" what to be attracted to or repelled by (but don't say that to a homophobe!). These reactions occur far, far below the level of "choosing."

Thus, when we sit test subjects down in a chair and monitor their brains as they are presented with images of things like a snake, a bleeding human hand, a pile of garbage, humans mating, maggots on steak, someone vomiting, a naked elderly person, surgery in progress - we will get very distinct and very honest results.

These results turn out to be highly accurate predictors of sociopolitical bias. Some patterns of attraction/revulsion predict liberal attitudes, some predict conservative attitudes.

The point being: we fall into these categories, not based on our "moral character" or "because we are smarter" or for any of the other (ridiculous) reasons we tell ourselves. We fall into these categories because we are born with different brains that receive the world in different ways.

This being the case, our squabbles seem all the more foolish, don't they?

(Turn to Page 43)

"We lived as hunter-gatherers for 99-plus percent of our history as human beings. So our feelings, our specifically human feelings, have been shaped in that environment. But we're not living in that environment anymore; and in particular we're living in environments where population densities are probably a hundred times, much more than a hundred times, greater than they were. So we're having to interact in a much more complex way with a much larger number of people than we're really properly evolved to do. And so there are going to be some difficulties."

~Vincent Sarich, UC Berkeley

Clustering in the USA

The cognitive clustering in the United States is extreme in a way it hasn't been since the Civil War. It is even safe to say that these are the only two times such a thing has occurred.

In Canada, there are five or six flavors of political bias - not just our two polar ones. In times past, of course (such as the Seventies), we shared that variety: there were many moderates in Congress; there were conservative Democrats and liberal Republicans.

This variety began weakening in the Reagan years, and received its death blow from Gingrich et al. From the late Eighties to the present moment, two heavy poles have been at work, drawing all in the middle - and their variety - to one pole or the other.

To survive, a mammal must seek out food, water, shelter, mates; it must also avoid predation and environmental danger. Too much attention to one and not enough attention to the other results in death.

Primates, however, are hyper-social creatures; we navigate the world collectively, not individually, and so we specialize, cognitively, by means of variable disposition: some are ultra-talented at Discovery, some ultra-talented at Security.

And between those two specializations lie many more subtle ones. Today, we are seeing that we truly are great apes: we have lost the sociopolitical variety that we spent decades cultivating, and have distilled back down to those two key groups: Discovery and Security.
For one group to try to dominate the other - let alone wipe it out - is species suicide.

The Framers, without the benefit of the anthropology and genetics, intuitively built a sociopolitical system that could accommodate cognitive variation - in fact, they provided a system that optimized it.Have we thrown that away?

(Turn to Page 74)

Human Natures

Most of our political antagonism over policy and incompatibilities between religious systems of thought boil down to differences in how we perceive human nature.

Over the past 12,000 years, we have created and institutionalized a variety of views of what human beings are and how they function inside. Many systems of law, many social frameworks have been designed around one person's or one group's ideas about the inner workings of a human being.

The Hebrew Old Testament and sections of the Koran stand out: they portray human beings as innately inclined toward evil, violence, greed, dishonesty, destruction. But they are by no means the only ones, and there is great variety in these views.

The truth is that *every* individual human views all other humans through a private (and frankly impossible) set of lenses, fine-tuned by in-group pressures and the lottery of personal experience. The point being, *no* human being has a complete innate grasp of human nature.

Our problem: creating systems of law and social institutions that allow for this wide variability, that do not impose any one particular take on human nature upon all people under its influence.

Is such a thing possible?

(Turn to Page 95)

How I See It is How It Isn't

How I See It Is How It Is is the very core of self-deception. No single human mind can begin to frame all of even its own immediate reality; we simply don't have the brain tissue for it.

We necessarily rely on others to inform our view, then. And we generally choose those in our proximity who see exactly the same things, which is the very height of stupidity, if an honest account of the world, our existence in it, and others around us is our goal.

The best that can be hoped for is *How We See It Is How It Is*, achieved with others of different or (better yet) skeptical view.

We have one, and only one, institution that sets this standard for refining the human view of self and reality: science. It is not perfect, but it is far, far more honest and accurate than our other institutions.

But that is not to say that we cannot create social communities whose collective efforts deliver a better-and-better view of self and world. I believe it can be done. I believe we've already achieved it - or, we did, 2,000 generations ago.

And we are, top to bottom, still the people today that we were back then. We can do this.

How Many Christs?

The Christ that the canonized Gospels presentis an amalgam of a number of different distinct (and sometimes mutually exclusive) personalities - that the character presented in the approved text is an invention-by-committee. This opens the door, the text being what it is, for people to look at Christ and see whomever they wish to see, or whomever they are instructed to see.

On the one hand, there is a Christ who is a soldier, a righteous, sword-bearing scourge who will one day return to blast the earth clean of those who do not bow to his father. He upholds all the Old Law, and is Authoritarian to the core. This Christ is deeply attractive to untold millions, and has been the model for many a human leader.

On the other hand, there is a Christ who is socialist to the core, a completely indiscriminate dispensary of healing and sustenance and equality, 'bringing down the mighty,' 'lifting up those of low degree' - a hippie Jesus, threatening to Authority and champion of the downtrodden. Untold millions flock to this Jesus, too, holding to his promise of 'Thy kingdom come... on earth.'

The point is this: whether we are talking Christ or some other figure we read about, historical or fictitious (in all candor, I take Christ to be fictitious), we see who we wish to see, because we zero in on traits in the character that resonate within ourselves. The truly great historical figures overwhelm those boundaries and force us to see beyond our resonance, as do those myths and figures who are exceptionally well-written (Othello, Odysseus, Willy Loman). But our deep emotional responses, in general, prevail.

When presented with a larger-than-life character, our brains tend to gravitate toward deep resonance and approval or deep revulsion and disapproval, depending on the structure of our individual brains. We laser-focus on those things we love or those things we hate.

But the truth is that every person around us, the mighty and the lowly, and every character we read of (among the well-conceived), all are made of more than those two emotional extremes. *All*human beings have a vast middle ground, not defined by arbitrary labels of Good and Evil, where they are just human beings.

When we focus on the facets of others that excite or repel us personally, we miss the human being beyond - and deprive ourselves of their true value.

(Turn to Page 130)

Partisanism

Partisanism is a binge of subjective gluttony. It clusters together those who already agree, absolving them of the rigors of validation, verification and justification. It discourages intellectual discipline as it promotes rationalization, eliminating the defense of ideas in favor of *ad hominem* refutations.

Partisanism rends our social fabric. It pulls apart the weave of thought and insight and viewpoint that bind a healthy, deliberative society. It rips apart minds in conference, dividing those who would otherwise bring ideas to market. It leaves the shroud of civilized discourse in tatters, unable to cover any of its adherents.

Partisanism weakens not only the group, but all of the constituents within. It softens the individual mind, relieving the need for deep scrutiny of self or others. It inspires an atrophy of empathy, curtailing our inborn reciprocities. It is deaf to the calls of reason, substituting a piper's tune of self-importance and imagined ethos. It casts aside the sharpening invigorations of confrontation and deliberation for easy vanities and empty congratulations.

Partisanism tears the social contract, pulling it apart shred by shred, as its enthusiasts toss aside all human commonalities with steadily mounting indifference, promoting themselves and demoting all others until no negotiations are possible. It dismisses obligation and enshrines privilege, exalting the arbitrary and eschewing the exigent.

Partisanism is hallucinogenic, invisible and odorless, populating the minds of its indulgents with self-aggrandizing illusions of moral rectitude and intellectual meliority. Its addicts see chimera who are not there, and can no longer see real people who are. It imbues faux beauty in one's cohorts, and even more faux pathos in those without. It inflates similarity within and difference beyond, like binoculars in a crowded room.

Partisanism is toxic. It fouls air shared by all. It nails door and window shut, burns away path and bridge. It creates animosities and hatreds out of nothing, pollutes discourse, makes enemies of colleagues, quarantines neighbors.

It spreads from mind to mind like empty song, crowding out meaning and reason and kinship. It stands alone among human inventions as the most phantasmal of weapons, made only of vacuous words - yet deadlier than plague.

(Turn to Page 182)

When You Assume…

Each human being carries within a full set of assumptions about self and others, a frame of human nature that was inherited from parents or peers or family or social tribe. These frames are taken for granted, as they are with us from early childhood and seldom challenged until adulthood.

All of our social behaviors and reactions to other people and groups are derived from those assumptions. *All* of our thinking about self and personal circumstance and potential future derive from those assumptions. *All* of our perspective on partnering, parenting, friendship and social obligation derive from those assumptions.

Most of those assumptions, given to us in childhood, came from religion or some other patriarchal hierarchy. *Most* of those assumptions paint human beings as naturally selfish, deceitful, hostile and violent. And thus begins a self-fulfilling prophecy that is now 500 generations old.

If those assumptions are bullshit – if we can replace them with a more objective, natural, scientific understanding of what human beings really are – then we can get out of the tar pit we're now trapped in, and get back to the good work of growing and evolving…

Empathy for the Human Race

Premise: human social order evolved over hundreds of thousands of years, then took a serious wrong turn at the end of the last ice age, about 12,000-14,000 years ago.

At that time, human beings radically changed lifestyle, transitioning from well-coordinated migratory hunting clans to settled agricultural communities. This has been well known for decades, but the study of the changes in human cognition that resulted are more recent. Anthropologists attribute hierarchical dominance, racism, misogyny and organized warfare to this fundamental shift. Why? Because we invented the concept of "property," the idea that individuals can own pieces of the world, that stored energy can be owned by one rather than all.

It became possible for one human being to control many, in opposition to the social framework of eons, that we survive through cooperation.

In short, throughout the relatively short term of "civilization," every human being born has lived and died within broken human community - no child entering the world has the opportunity to live in natural cooperation with others, by way of our evolutionary path.

And since we can survive together in groups of tens of thousands, rather than the naturally prescribed dozens, we can cluster into unhealthy cognitive groups, truncating our social wisdom and curtailing our natural tendency to cooperate for our mutual benefit.

It's the easiest thing in the world to point at other social groups and consider them broken, to put them down and call them less than we are. But it isn't they who are broken - it is human community; those who exist in groups other than our own aren't less - merely different, heirs to different brains, different genes.

Bad enough to have those who naturally possess less propensity for empathy to be doing this finger-pointing, but far worse to see it among those to whom nature bequeathed a great deal of empathy. The former, we can understand; the latter are without excuse.

There is much to criticize in the current march of human affairs, a great deal that needs to change. But as risk and threat increase, empathy and understanding are wavering. When we stop segmenting human beings into these terrible categories and look at them as a whole, surely we can recover a little of both...

(Turn to Page 60)

Yes, I Mind...

Yes, I mind your ignorance; it removes a useful voice from the human chorus.

Yes, I mind your ideology; your Me-and-Mine behaviors threaten not only those beyond your circle, but humans the world over (not to mention you and yours).

Yes, I find your behavior offensive; your endless shaming of Those Not Like You is an affront to every ancestor who walked an extra day, birthed another infant, fought off a leopard with a stick and wondered over the stars.

Yes, I realize it isn't your fault; your brain contains more tissue where discomfort lives and less tissue where conflict resolution is performed. You are not worse and those not like you are not better – it's the luck of the draw... but you are, ironically, less likely to accept the truth of that than they are.

Yes, I think you are dangerous; when those like you rise up, you stir all that is worst in the human psyche, igniting emotions that shouldn't even exist in our species. You threaten those who have done you no harm and would welcome and accept you without a second thought, but for your endless aggression.

No, I'm not going to do anything about you; to try to silence you would be to adopt your backward ways, which are ineffective in any case. To try to end you, as your tribe has ended so many over the centuries, would be futile – you're in our genes! – and would make me a traitor to our species.

But I will do everything in my power to keep you *out* of power, where your maladapted and toxic view of humanity has done so much harm. My reasons above are many, but more simply – you don't know very much and you don't think very well.

How to Walk Away

I had known my conservative friend for many years. We had served in the same Fundamentalist church together. I remember arguments with him about Bill Clinton we'd had over lunch at Burger King, in the actual Clinton years.

"How can you walk away?" he asked me earnestly. "You're turning your back on God. You're deciding you can do just fine without Him. Worse, you're telling the world that you think you're better than the rest of us."

I couldn't just give him a quick, canned answer. I would have to really tell him.

"That turns out not to be the case," I told him.

"I walked away from religion because it required me to be less good than I wish to be.

"I will not treat women the way the Evangelical church would have me treat them. I will not be part of an institution that requires me to despise people I know to be good, while excusing people I know to be evil. I can be a much better man beyond the church than within it.

"I walked away from right-wing politics, though I was raised hard-core GOP, because those politics are dishonest – unfair, by design, to those who are not within the circle. They are the politics of exclusion, and I am uncomfortable with the dishonesty and the unfairness. I am more free to be just and honest beyond the GOP.

"I walked away from conservatism because it does not reflect the innate value of every human being. It is a toxic representation of human nature – a cynical, ugly view of what human beings are and why they do what they do and feel what they feel. Even if science had not utterly refuted your craven, depraved vision of humankind (which it has), I would *still* reject it, because it is so unloving and innately disrespectful. I can embrace a more accurate and productive model of human nature beyond the confines of conservatism.

"Finally, I walked away because I could not remain among you and be who I really am. Your casual disregard of science is childish and cowardly; and science tells me that my 'moral' choices and 'value' judgments are limbic emotional responses, not the product of ethical self-confrontation. I see 'Others' differently than you do because our brains are different; the 'values' you go on and on about are a result of differences in our brains, gifts of our genes. When you call me 'libtard,' you may as well be calling me 'nigger' or 'faggot.' (And the same is true of my liberal friends who say 'Repuglican'.)"

"I walked away because I just cannot be one of you. I wish you could see the love and friendship that exists in the decades I tried to."

(Turn to Page 172)

Lamentation for Goldilocks

It isn't enough that Earth is a "Goldilocks planet," neither too hot nor too cold, with plenty of liquid water and gaseous oxygen; it is as beholden to its grossly oversized satellite for the existence of life within its thin surface layers, a moon that churns its oceans; it is as beholden to its inherent radiation shield, a fortuitous concentration of ozone in its upper atmosphere; and to its off-kilter axial tilt, which cycles the energy pouring inward from the sun in an extended polyrhythm with its rapid rotation, driving evolution as significantly as the stirring of the oceans.

Within the agonizingly thin layers of liquid and gas enshrouding its global form there emerge vanishingly small concatenations of carbon-bearing molecules, machines with built-in memory that harvest and release the energy of the sun, in concert with air and water. Islands of heat form and dissipate, and machines give rise to larger machines, with ever-larger memory and greater complexity.

There finally emerge self-propelled particles within these clouds, energy-bearing particles who see, hear, feel, and wonder, breaking down and rebuilding the Earth, making the universe aware.

These energy-bearing particles are unique in time and space, their fragility offset by their magnificence as crucibles of self-awareness. They have the capacity to reshape the Earth and eventually the stars.

That will turn out not to be the case. They only consume each other.

"Our way of thinking – both individually and collectively – is dominated by short-term horizons and distorted by habits of thought inherited from our prehistoric ancestors, who had to survive threats very different from the ones we face today."

~Al Gore, *The Future*

Starbuck (or Space: The Female Frontier)[4]

In my late youth, there was *Battlestar: Galactica*, a prime-time children's program about hotshot space pilots trying to save humanity from the products of its own folly. Sort of like *Doctor Who*, minus the brains and charm. My favorite character on that show was Starbuck – a cigar-chomping, card-playing, womanizing rogue who was always throwing himself in danger's path because he had so little to lose, cracking jokes as he went.

Fast forward to 2003, when Ron Moore recreates Galactica as all too adult – dark, disturbing, an allegory of our post-9/11 culture, packed with unsettling metaphors and reflections of ourselves we'd rather not see. And this time around, Starbuck is a woman.

And *what* a woman! Played with an in-your-face energy and smoldering anger by Katie Sakhoff, Starbuck – Kara Thrace – is once again the cigar-chomping, card-playing rogue, the very best of the best at what she does – intelligent, bold, stronger than any man around her, and very, very damaged.

Damaged?

Yes, damaged. The original 1978 Starbuck (Dirk Benedict) had his issues – abandonment, primarily – but Kara Thrace is a veritable encyclopedia of pathologies, not the least of which is a desperate self-loathing that derives largely (but not exclusively) from an oppressive guilt she suffers, having carelessly sent her lover to his death.

So why does she have to be damaged?

In all fairness, every character on the show, male or female, is deeply damaged. That's part of the point of the show. And we will talk about damage here today.

I call my youngest daughter Starbuck. She and I are very close, and have been all her brief life. We spend lots of time together, week in and week out.

[4] Originally published in the blog "That Turns Out Not to Be the Case," Sept. 10, 2013

We cook together, watch *The Big Bang Theory* together. I've educated her well, introducing her to *Star Wars, Lord of the Rings, Trek, Doctor Who*, all the good stuff. She's just now getting into Dungeons and Dragons, and she's a talented cartoonist. She took up golf just this summer, and is already within eight strokes of my score, every time we play.

Years ago, she told me she had every intention of becoming the first female US president. She was only slightly miffed when I gently informed her that Hillary Clinton was going to beat her by several decades (a prediction overcome by the events of 2016).

Why is he telling us this?

While I could brag on my awesome daughter all day and night, I'm telling you this because she's just the pinnacle of an abundant number of smart, talented, beautiful women in my world. And another of those women recently brought to my attention an issue which tugs my thoughts firmly in the direction of my daughter's future.

My friend published a link to a video that featured a heart-rending poetry reading, and its substance was to do with the manner in which Western culture minimizes women – not just conceptually, but in the physical world. Women are taught, passively, spatial timidity.

Men are taught the opposite – to own the space they occupy, to project power, to consider the space they're sitting or standing in to be "territory." But a woman lives with the passive assumption that the space she occupies is borrowed – not hers to own. Consequently, a man will expand to fill his space, whether on the sidewalk, on a bus, sitting in a restaurant – while a woman will shrink, pulling arms and legs inward, containing herself. Men tend to spread their arms out, stretch their legs. Women tend not to use the armrests in a movie theater.

The feminist rant over this phenomenon is well justified: this subconscious impulse that burdens the woman is a reflection of a social status that's unjust, indefensible, flat-out wrong. And it's just an echo of status issues we see all around us, if we open our eyes.

For instance, in the geek world I've opened up to my daughter, there's the problem of the female superhero. Author Michael Chabon does a wonderful riff on this one, pointing out that Wonder Woman has no narrative of her own whatsoever; that Superman's younger cousin Supergirl is utterly deferential; and that even in the Legion of Super-Heroes, where nearly half the heroes are women, the reflections are of every demeaning prejudice a bunch of male writers could muster: one of these female heroes has the power of shrinking to nothing, one becomes insubstantial. Even in the Fantastic Four, the female's power is to … turn invisible.

But back to the space problem. It's not that men are doing a bad thing, spreading their arms wide, stretching their legs; it's that *women have as much right as men to claim their space*. And in fairness to men, the space thing isn't about women – it's about *other men*. The territoriality of men isn't intended as a dominance over women; it's intended as competition between men.

The insult to women is that they aren't allowed into that competition. It's easy to reduce this to a cliche, to claim that this is the nature of men and women, that the subjugation of women is How It's Always Been.

But that turns out not to be the case.

Forget everything you think you know about cavepeople. Forget what "the Bible says." Patriarchy is a human invention, not a natural state; and it's a fairly recent invention, in the scheme of things. While it's certainly true that men have dominated women throughout recorded history, remember that recorded history represents far less than ten percent of *homo sapiens* history. Before the advent of agriculture, when everything went to hell, men and women were far more equal than they are today.

Did you know, for instance, that digs in my native Kentucky have given us evidence that in many tribes, some of the finest hunters were *women*? And don't bother squabbling over it – that's still true today, among the Anmatyerre of Northern Australia.

We have strong evidence that women in prehistory were flat-out smarter – that women invented clothing … rope … basketry … pottery – while the patents of prehistoric men were pretty much limited to weapons. There is even tentative evidence that *language itself* is a female innovation.

Women did not become the property of men, and consequently unentitled to the space they occupy, until the concept of *property* evolved – and that was only 12,000 years ago. In the previous 100,000 years, men and women were team players.

Sandi Copeland, an adjunct professor in the department of anthropology at the University of Colorado, has noted that in primate societies we observe today, it is the *females,* rather than the males, who tend to be more exploratory. Arguing that this is a productive sexual impulse that combats the effects of inbreeding, Copeland indicts men as couch-hugging butt-scratchers as far back as 2.7 million years. And lest we fight the notion that this idea applies to early humans – we know from laser ablations and strontium isotope analyses of hominid teeth that females, rather than males, tended to travel much farther from their natal groups.

Put simply: until men developed the capacity to hold power over each other in large groups, women not only had as much power as men – they out-performed them.

So where does this leave Starbuck?

My daughter already radiates more power and potential than I ever did, and faces greater opportunity than I ever had. If I've contributed, apart from my time and my geek library, it's been through a simple mantra I've repeated since she was a toddler ...*pretty face ... smart brains ... kind heart!*

... and I've told her endlessly that those features, which she possesses in abundance, are listed in ascending order of importance.

But there needs to be more.

The world we've created is tough enough for a woman to navigate without worrying over elbow room at dinner or movie theater armrests. However much power my daughter claims for herself, entering a patriarchal culture rigged for her male peers, it's going to be offset to an unfair degree. Her success and happiness are my deepest desires; it's on me to open every door I can for her, to model proper male attitude and deference, to build her up every single day, and to send her back into the game every time she's knocked down with my most earnest encouragement.

And I have to stick with this in the shadow of my own endless failings in this arena – pushing past all the times I took more than my share, thoughtlessly neglected to offer a woman her due, or took excessive umbrage to an affront of which I myself was all the guiltier.

I've already made clear to her that her thoughts are her own and she doesn't need my permission to think them. In any and all matters, from religion to sex and everything in between, she should make up her own mind, even (and especially) when her ideas are at odds with mine – and that the only deference her mother and I insist on will be in matters of health and safety. Is that enough? Probably not, but it's a start. The real challenge for me is living up to the standard I am telling her is her birthright – to claim my space, but never at the expense of anyone else's – especially a woman's.

Starbuck is about to turn 13. I'll be giving her a box of cigars.

And I'll be campaigning for her in 2048.

The Myth of the Ditzy Female

Misogyny is not only unnatural, it is a cognitive and emotional perversion, destructive to the men who practice it, the women they practice it on, and all who are exposed to such exchanges - including children.

Our cracking of the human genome has given us deep insights into gender status in prehistory. Women, not men, were in charge of reproduction, and thus had a defining role in social structures. Women were anything but property then - a situation that changed when the Ice Age ended, and we invented the ideas of property and ownership, and learned how to dominate one another - women being first in line.

It is a foregone conclusion that the Myth of the Ditzy Female - the idea that women were intellectually inferior to men (a myth that persisted all the way into the 20th century!) - is a social dominance plank with no basis in reality. Now that we understand it to be false, we can proceed to dismantle the remaining lies about women - and restore them to their rightful place in the Human Story.

To Be Understood

I suppose it's fair to say that the things we've said about how human minds and social groups function might be a bit discouraging, on this front: if people tend to filter their experience of others through these complex brain interactions, how in the world can we hope to be seen clearly?

That is, certainly, one of the defining conundrums of the human condition.

The answer is obviously not found in our political process, or our social biases, or our religious rhetoric - all of these things taint our perceptions of others. They are group reflections of our individual social frames. They don't help, they hinder.

Imagine the following: Ten of us are standing in a circle, and someone is standing in the middle. I pass around a box of pairs of glasses. Each pair has smudges on its lenses, and the smudges vary, pair to pair. If we all look at the guy in the middle, no one of us will see him clearly, we will all see him incompletely - but together, we are taking in all there is to see. Together, we have a strong sense of the person the man in the middle is.

This same phenomenon describes all of our social perception. Even in our most intimate setting - the family - neither parent sees the child completely; the two parents together, combining their perceptions, construct the deepest portrait of the child. And even then, that portrait can be informed by the perceptions of the child's siblings.

If we want to be understood, then, our best bet is Community. We are seen most clearly when we open ourselves not just to our partner, not just to our family, but to community - to share our inner self with an array of others, each of whom will pick up and appreciate different bits and pieces of who we are - and reflect back, in sum, who we really are.

Empathy in the Modern Era

Human beings vary in their natural reservoirs of empathy, as empathy is a neurological phenomenon. We are born with a predisposition to some greater or lesser amount of it, and that predisposition is either cultivated or resisted by our upbringing, in-group and life experience.

Here's the thing: whatever end of the spectrum one finds oneself, when it comes to personal capacity for empathy - from 0 (the sociopath) to 11 (the Bleeding Heart) - the level within us is what we consider "normal", meaning that everyone who has less or more than we do is viewed as abnormal. And we proceed to hold either their deficiency or excess against them.

Western culture - and capitalism, in particular - greatly diminish our natural levels of empathy. Deep identification with others, as a default, inhibits competition and bolsters that sense of the good of all over the good of self - not exactly good news for a society ostensibly geared toward the cultivation of individualism. Empathy is on the ropes in the modern era.

So once again, I'll turn to the distant past and argue that in ancient human tribes, our empathy was pooled: we were always in the moment together, so whatever befell any one of us, there was empathy enough.

Wouldn't it be great if it could be like that again?

(Turn to Page 87)

Golden Apples: Ray Bradbury and Me

It's the mid-Seventies, and I'm about to stumble into Ray Bradbury.

The setting for this meeting could not be more perfect. I'm a seventh grader sitting in study hall, on the third floor of an ancient rural Indiana school building. In the early part of the 20th century, this was a high school, one of those antiquated temples with very high ceilings, wide staircases with thick oaken bannisters, red brick façade and a gymnasium straight out of *Hoosiers*. Fifty years later, there's a brand-spanking-new high school 10 miles away, and this old building is now a junior high school.

We glide back in time every morning, me and my friends, on a weary yellow school bus, through endless cornfields, past trees and farmhouses, grain silos and ponds. This little town sits a few hours south of the rural Illinois terrain of Ray's own youth, and even though I don't know any of this yet, it is soon going to feel very real to me. I'm about to be pulled across time, in both directions, and through pure chance, I'm starting the journey in exactly the right space.

The study hall is, appropriately, right next to the library. As far as I'm concerned, that truly does make this old place a temple.

I raise my hand silently. The teacher on duty, used to this signal, nods. I quietly leave my seat and vanish into the stacks.

I emerge with a thick volume – *S is for Space* – and take my seat again. I flip to the second story – "Pillar of Fire" – and everything changes for me. My first bite from the first golden apple is ostensibly science fiction – the story of a 20th century man accidentally revived in the 24th – but it's more horror, as this fellow feeds on fear and death, and sets about re-introducing them both into the sterile, clean future in which he finds himself. More than that, it's a psychological thriller, as Ray invites me into this creature's mind, and the mind of his 24th century pursuer.

And there's a second bite, and a third, and a fourth – "Come Into My Cellar", "Zero Hour", "The Pedestrian" – and I find to my delight, upon later visiting the town library, that there are many, many more golden apples.

That summer, my feet leave the earth for days on end, as I devour *The Martian Chronicles*, *The Illustrated Man*, *Fahrenheit 451*. And when my feet do touch earth again, it is now more magical than the sky – a place where time and youth now stand still, something out of *Dandelion Wine*, a barefoot odyssey through shadowy woods and dusty cellars, echoing with the twilight calls of parents from porches as elderly neighbors scowl through windows.

This eccentric, inexplicable bond between small-town youth and the grand sweep of space and time is the stuff of Twain, carried into the modern age, past and future intertwining with no real rhyme or reason but abundant romance. Robots on horseback.Stained-glass windows into mind. I'm off and running, and though I've been reading science fiction and fantasy since grade school, I've never met anyone like Ray.

My feel for this magical difference comes quickly, and in a few years I'll understand it intellectually, but it's apparent from those earliest readings. Isaac offers thoughts and ideas, Arthur serves up grand concepts. Robert presents eccentric personalities. But Ray – Ray paints wondrous pictures, so real and compelling and authentic that the world around me melts into them. The Big Three draw me to worlds I love to visit; Ray's, I never want to leave.

My passages to Terminus and Jupiter and Tertius all came to me by way of John W. Campbell, Jr., editor of the seminal *Astounding Science Fiction* before and during the war years. Heinlein, Clarke and Asimov, by way of *Astounding*, were launched to such heights that their names became well-known beyond the pimpled fraternity of boys like me, famous the world over. Significantly, Ray Bradbury was the only science fiction name known to the general public who was *not* a Campbell discovery; he emerged in Los Angeles rather than New York (where *Astounding* was based), brought into the fold by Forrest J. Ackerman (who, God bless him, bought my first story when I was but 14 years of age. Perry Rhodan #102. Run, don't walk!).

Campbell's emphasis on realistic science and strong plotting and character development did much to raise science fiction out of its juvenile origins and into the mainstream; but Bradbury's surreal, romantic style was far afield of the reason-driven fare of Campbell's authors, and expanded the genre's appeal farther than they ever could have. People who never went near science fiction magazines at all nonetheless read *The Martian Chronicles* and *Fahrenheit 451*. Ray's work was the first to be regarded by the general public as *literature*, not just genre.

His titles alone could carry us across that gulf; only Harlan Ellison compares, in the knack of finding a perfect (and often lengthy) memorable title that sets the ideal tone for the work beneath. "Dark They Were, and Golden-Eyed"; "Something Wicked This Way Comes"; "I Sing the Body Electric"; "The Golden Apples of the Sun"; "There Will Come Soft Rains" … titles so romantic and lyrically metered that they take up residence in memory right away, and never leave.

They hurl us into the terrors of childhood, the dread of death, the uncertainties of time, the warmth of family, the joys of our dreams, the darkness of our unspoken thoughts. We experience the heat of the veldt, the churning dark waters around the lighthouse; we take in the violet grasses of Mars, the sinister faces in the carnival, the scaled monsters of the Cretaceous.

But Ray's stuff does more than launch us into confrontation with those things within us that are magical and dark and longing; it keeps us anchored as it goes, not only teasing at what we might be but reminding us who we are. It isn't just nostalgia he's working here – it's an understanding, a constant homage, an on-going celebration of that elemental force in that third-floor study hall that pulls a young mind into the stacks, that reconciliation of light and dark, of glow and shadow – the idea that who we are and who we can become are not distinct propositions, but of a piece.

Just after I learned Ray had died, I asked him about this.

"We are the miracle of force and matter, making itself over into imagination and will," he said. "Incredible! The Life Force experimenting with forms. You for one. Me for another. The Universe has shouted itself alive, and we are one of the shouts."

So, I said, basically all this time you've been repeating the shout?

"If you enjoy living, it is not difficult to keep the sense of wonder," he said. "We are cups, constantly and quietly being filled. The trick is knowing how to tip ourselves over and let the beautiful stuff out."

Maybe, I said – I sure hope he's right about this – But sometimes it's hard to get there from here.

"You've got to jump off cliffs," he answered, "and build your wings on the way down."

Thanks, Ray, I say, and then I tell him about that long-ago third-floor study hall. And it's here that Ray and I find our deepest, most permanent connection – the infinite adventure of the printed word, the musty glory of those ancient temples.

"Go find your bliss," he tells me, "Name your favorites and see if your long umbilical memory has been cut or you are still wonderfully tied to the things you loved in libraries long ago … "

In the summer of 1991, I took my children to see that Indiana school building where Ray and I first met. It wasn't there; not a single brick remained. I was devastated, and the only remedy was to take the kids to the park, buy them an ice cream, and recreate it for them, summoning it back into existence with stories – to bridge the time and space between, as Ray did, unceasingly.

And it dawned on me, when I got to the part about Ray and the third-floor study hall, that *because* of Ray, I've had that power all along. Until Ray left us last week, I assumed that this wondrous magic emanated from him, that without him the light would die out, that the third-floor study hall would slip away into time, not a brick remaining …

… but that turns out not to be the case.

Touch

Human beings - all primates, really, and a number of other mammals - have within them a "moral molecule," a peptide hormone called oxytocin. This substance evolved in order to facilitate mammalian life itself (though earlier forms exist in virtually all vertebrates), having among its functions the triggering of phases of childbirth and lactation reflexes.

Oxytocin is touch-triggered. The touching of the female breasts, after childbirth, triggers lactation; the stroking of the infant cheek triggers the turning of her head, a latch motion.

But Nature is often casual in craft, and our capacity to produce oxytocin persists beyond the acts of birthing and feeding. Touch is a bonding mechanism in the full array of human relationships, from the embrace of lovers to the handshake of colleagues, from the tumbling of children to the chest-bump of linebackers. The well-being triggered by the release of oxytocin has been repurposed in countless ways, and as tactile creatures with little hair, we are able to release it at will, and in great amounts.

It was Paul Zak[5] who dubbed it "the moral molecule," making the case that the human capacity for touch is the foundation of human bonding. And, sure enough, that argument stands strong when we consider the circumstances of our evolution - traveling constantly in extended families, few if any reasons to withhold contact.

We've built a social universe that constrains touch considerably, so that we experience the slightest fraction of what our forgotten grandparents experienced. As a result, our bonds are both far fewer and far weaker. Moreover, our society is structured in such a way as to perpetuate this condition.

It is not a great leap to wonder why this is so - to consider that keeping distance between us, by design, serves the ends of those who profit from human isolation. There is little we can do, apart from incremental gains in our day-to-day encounters - and wonder what we've missed.

---

[5]*The Moral Molecule: The New Science of What Makes Us Good and Evil*, Paul Zak.

We Decided It for Ourselves

The noted endocrinologist Robert Sapolsky, one of neuroscience's most engaging and effective evangelists, makes the point that armchair theorists like Marlin Perkins did much to mis-educate the public on how genetics work. Perkins, on several occasions, presented the deaths of elderly herd animals as self-sacrifice for the greater good, arguing that it was a built-in trait.

Genes do not favor groups, Sapolsky corrects in his popular courses, genes only favor their couriers. That being the case, how do we justify the concept of cognitive differentiation (many minds together) as a genetic boon?

The answer is, we decided it for ourselves (human beings, that is). Our brains, and therefore our differing styles of thought, will always be randomized, by the mechanics of genetics - but without design.

What human beings did was something no creature had done before - leverage the differences to mutual advantage. *All* mammals are going to show genetically randomized variation in volume of brain components - but *none* demonstrate group behaviors driven by those variations.

In short, our increasing propensity for social behavior gave survival value to random brain characteristics - and thus, we survived, and thrived, with greater success than any of our predecessors or cousins.

The key: *We decided it for ourselves*. We can do that again.

Letting Go of Political Rage

Progressives, liberals and mainstream Dems all pay more attention to (and have more respect for) science than their right-wing counterparts, for reasons that science itself clarifies. But we are no more in a position to cherry-pick the products of science than they are; you accept that science delivers honest, best-we-can-do-today answers, or you scrap it and go mystical.

Increasingly, digital technology and brain imaging are unwrapping the secrets of how our minds work, and the more we learn, the less we have to get upset about, politically or otherwise: our thoughts, our feelings, our perceptions and our decisions are far less acts of will than we suppose, and we are far more indebted to our genes and the nuances of our experience and environment than we ever might have believed, in the less enlightened past.

Put another way, we aren't nearly as in charge of our thoughts and emotions as we think we are; we aren't even, for the most part, all that aware of where they come from. We don't "choose" our point of view, or our attitudes, or even our values; they choose us.

This is especially true of our social brains, the thoughts and feelings and attitudes we have about self and others - thoughts and feelings that form the core of our political viewpoints. We are predisposed to experience other human beings in different ways - to accept different assumptions about the nature of human beings, their behaviors, their motivations, for reasons having nothing to do with the reality behind those behaviors and motivations. And when we note that someone has this different set of assumptions, we tend to judge them, to look down on them or dismiss them because they do not see as clearly as we believe we do.

Science has weighed in, and the findings are that this condescension is inappropriate. We can no more judge another person for having social biases that are the polar opposite of our own than we can judge them for having dark skin; we can no more impugn their values and morality for their distance from our own than we can demean homosexuals for not sharing our bedroom preferences.

Our sociopolitical predispositions are not a matter of choice; they are a matter of brain chemistry. And when it comes to science, we can't have it both ways. We can't parade the objective reality science illuminates and then set it aside when it interferes with our outrage; we have to conform to truth wherever it leads us. And it's leading us to a more complete understanding of why our social chasms exist, and why they grow as quickly and disastrously as they do.

Our outrage does nothing to bridge those gaps; our sense of superiority leads us away from resolution, not toward it; our "values" own far more to the lottery of birth than to our imagined moral fortitude.

Should we be outraged over the actions of those in power, when those actions threaten us? Of course. When they play fast and loose with public policy in such a way as to risk our lives, we *should* feel rage. But there's a vast difference between being outraged over the danger to ourselves and others and cultivating a loathing for those who would change the world to conform to their view - we, after all, are trying to do exactly the same thing, and we are as subject to the roulette of cognitive diversity as they.

Christians have a saying, one that they don't really practice but which nonetheless contains a core of truth: "Hate the sin, love the sinner." This is what I propose. No single human mind can get the world right in isolation - and grouped minds tend to perform poorly when they all think the same thoughts. Our species needs to return to that rich diversity, to tear down our echo chambers and learn to enjoy those who are different, once again. Our faux rage and imagined superiority are obstructing that course. Let's do something about that. We can welcome and even celebrate those who are different while remaining vigilant about seeking out the political course that is ultimately best for all. It's not an either/or choice.

"I don't want my thoughts to die with me, I want to have done something. I'm not interested in power, or piles of money. I want to leave something behind. I want to make a positive contribution – know that my life has meaning."

~Temple Grandin

Golden Rules

"But I say unto you, Love your enemies; pray for those who persecute you." This verse from the Sermon on the Mount, from the more socialist version of Christ, has always inspired interest for its antithetical human sentiment, over-the-top altruism and screaming illogic. On the one hand, yes, far better to repay antagonism with kindness; on the other, to not resist in the face of aggression is to be consumed by it.

We know where the Christian Right stands on this verse; not only do they not stand down in the face of aggression - nine times out of ten they *are* the aggression.

We've accounted for this in the cognitive diversity frame; it is not to do with a lack of spiritual integrity or excessive aggression - it is a genetically-derived social discomfort driven by communication between brain components that Hebrew writers failed to account for.

Even so, the verse itself is very illuminating, and should not be dismissed.

Though there are many voices speaking in the canonized Gospel text, the Sermon on the Mount voice is tapping into what I guess we might call 'paleospirituality': how human beings related to one another and treated one another, tens of thousands of years before the ideas of gods and holy texts. And the portrait we see, in this verse and many others, is that of a species in solidarity.

We see human beings as described in the mountainside sermon, in unity, cooperation, mutual consideration; in emotional purity, with regard to one another; in praise of empathy, untainted by the toxins of inequality.

That same sermon also goes frighteningly authoritarian in places, but this central theme remains clear: there is a pervasive thread, in human beings, that a part of our ancestral memories preserve this pre-civilized state, when our survival depended upon our acceptance of and cooperation with *all* others of our kind. This text and many other snippets of those memories, sprinkled through the historical record and our ancient literature, give us hope that we can unbox those memories and find ways to breathe life into them...

Passengers

The sci-fi movie *Passengers* tells the story of two people on a huge starship, a colonization mission carrying thousands of sleeping immigrants. During its 120-year flight, the starship is quiet, as both the passengers and crew are in suspended animation, while the ship is piloted by computer.

The first of the two people, Jim (Chris Pratt), is awakened accidentally. He spends more than a year in total isolation, a loneliness underscored by the ship's vast spaces - there are huge concourses and malls and chambers everywhere, nothing but space all around him, and all of it empty of other faces and voices.

With only an android bartender for company, Jim begins to lose it - he comes within a heartbeat of ejecting himself into space. Finally, he persuades himself to awaken another passenger, Aurora (Jennifer Lawrence), to end his solitude.

The thing is - they are still 90 years from their destination. They will both die before the starship reaches the colony planet for which it is bound. In his need for companionship, he has essentially taken her life away from her.

The ethical issue is clear - and when Aurora learns what he has done, she is rightfully enraged.

The thing is - who among us can judge him? Who among us, faced with decades of total solitude, wouldn't begin to lose ourselves, to unravel inside?

In the end, it all works out for the best: had Jim not been awakened, had he not likewise awakened Aurora, the starship would have exploded, and all would have died in any case. The outcome, in the end, was the best possible.

Still, the story's ideas bring home the truth that human beings are simply not built for solitude. We are social beings, created to each be part of a greater whole, to participate in a human experience beyond self. Our individual minds can take in a great deal, but it is among others of our kind that the meaning of our experience expands and deepens.

Morality in Cognitive Clusters

Within a cognitive cluster - a social group made up of people of the same or similar cognitive types - assumptions about human nature and what is and isn't "moral" tend to be held by every group member. Group membership often hinges on this acceptance of group thinking.

Our jaws drop when we hear of House Majority Leader Kevin McCarthy and Speaker Paul Ryan talking with other GOP leaders about Putin and Trump, and saying:

> McCarthy: "There's... there's two people, I think, Putin pays: Rohrabacher and Trump...[laughter]...Swear to God."

> Ryan: "This is an off the record...[laughter]...No leaks...[laughter]...alright? This is how we know we're a real family here."

> Scalise: "That's how you know that we're tight."

> [laughter]

> Ryan: "What's said in the family stays in the family."

It seems despicable, and sure enough, we find ourselves loathing them. But this behavior is a reflection of a moral code that is perfectly natural for some cognitive types: their brains are built for in-group loyalty; protecting their 'clan' is the highest service.

Similarly, remember George Lakoff's description of how 'truth' and 'lies' work in the Authoritarian follower's mind: "It doesn't matter if Trump lies to them, and they know he's lying, because there's a higher truth – which is Strict Father Morality itself, which has consequences, and they are truer than any lies – and that if you deny that, if you accept the lies as more important, you're denying your self-identity. That's why there are 'alternative facts'."

And there's Senate Majority Leader McConnell, who openly places his party's interests ahead of the national interest (his claim would be that there is no distinction).

My point is this: it would be crazy to expect anything else. The perception among some social groups that defense of the group, loyalty to the group, constitutes the overriding moral choice is natural - it is how they view the social universe. When Paul Ryan invokes the word 'family,' it isn't hyperbole; that's truly what he means. Party-as-family. And we stick by our family, even when they're wrong, even when they're despicable.

This doesn't mean we excuse or go along with the behaviors that follow from this thinking; by definition, it is fractured thinking, the product of cognitive clustering. It is toxic to society as a whole, and corrosive to our national institutions. But it *does* mean that we can dial down the contempt. These are not 'bad' people; they are just people, wading through a social swamp that every one of us is born into and ensnared by till we die. We can be wary of behaviors and negative outcomes without indulging in hatred and contempt for those who are no more or less trapped and hobbled as we ourselves.

(Turn to Page 134)

Neolithic Inequality

Imagine, for a moment, that our distant ancestors adopted our economics...

Chuck and Roger and Jessica and Betty have all now settled, along with their clan of 120, in a small river valley in the Fertile Crescent. There is plenty of fresh water, the weather is mild, and they have constructed huts for sleeping and pens for raising animals.

There are several small fields of grain that they tend, and having invented pottery, they have large jars of grain stacked in huts for the purpose. There is a small structure at the edge of the village for the slaughtering of meat, and a large fire pit.

Chuck, Roger, Jessica and Betty all participate in the cultivation and preparation of this village wealth. In a typical year, their individual compensation for their labor comes to 260 pounds of meat, 14 jars of wheat, 150 gallons of fresh water and five bags of fruit and assorted roots and plants.

Lloyd is the clan's leader. His recently-negotiated annual compensation for overseeing agro and livestock operations is 117,000 pounds of meat, 6,300 jars of wheat, 67,500 gallons of fresh water and 2,250 bags of fruit and assorted roots and plants.

In the event that the clan votes Lloyd out as leader, he will receive a severance/retirement package totaling 1,625,000 pounds of meat, 87,500 jars of wheat, 937,500 gallons of fresh water and 31,250 bags of fruit and assorted roots and plants. Moreover, he will be permitted to retain the private use of a donkey for personal transportation.

Chuck, Roger, Jessica, Betty and their 120 kinspeople are not crazy about this arrangement, but the village's board of directors signed off on it, so what can they do?

The directors, by the way, serve no function other than to be directors, devoting one hour a month to the task. Their annual compensation for this effort comes to 1,300 pounds of meat, 70 jars of wheat, 750 gallons of fresh water and 25 bags of fruit and assorted roots and plants.

Chuck, Roger, Jessica and Betty are not crazy about that, either, but hey - they get Sundays off, so who's complaining?

(Turn to Page 200)

Ranting for Science

I grew up in a deeply Fundamentalist household, but never fit in - the reasons for that are, at this point, clear, and we don't need to revisit them. But my interest in science took hold early on: I was reading Asimov's science essays at 10 or 11, developing interests in chemistry and astronomy soon after, and cultivated a personal enthusiasm for the space program and the emerging technology of computers in the mid-Seventies. My parents were tolerant and even supportive of all of this, and my love of *Star Trek* - so long as I didn't believe in evolution.

From that day to this, my devotion to science has grown a thousand-fold, and my belief that it is the key to the benign humanist future has only intensified.

But along the way, my childhood tribe's opposition to evolution has grown into a full-blown distrust and antagonism toward science in general, and this antagonism is as much upon me.

What the Right has done, in fostering doubt about not only the product but the very nature of science is not only disingenuous, not merely dishonorable, but an act of aggression against humankind altogether. It is a denial of our finest accomplishment, for the petty and puny purpose of self-enrichment and aggrandizement. It is the discarding of real pearls for the substitution of plastic fakes. It is the discarding of reality for self-pampering illusions.

Science is the path back to our more honest selves, the highway forward into a healthier and more secure future; it is the great equalizer, the solution to Authoritarianism, our hedge against the manipulations of elites. Science bows to no man, and frees us all from bowing.

Science restores us to a place of honest confrontation with the universe, protecting us from our personal emotions while stretching our individual minds beyond all personal limitations; it forces us to acknowledge what is real and let go of what is not; it insists that we cooperate, that we work together, that we accomplish in concert; it builds bridges of shared understanding, a staircase to the stars, while tearing down walls of deceit and fear.

It is deserving of our respect and participation, and utterly undeserving of the Right's attempts to misrepresent, devalue and demean it.

My youngest child - who just blew through the remake of *Cosmos* this month! – will March For Science with me soon. It may be the most important thing I do this year.

Threat-scanners Gotta Scan

Threat-scanners do not simply threat-scan - so committed are they to the activity, so existentially necessary do they see threat-scanning to be, that they teach others to do it, and create systems of thought and social interaction that have Threat-scanning baked in.

This is the core of, among other institutions, patriarchal religion. It is the nature of patriarchy in general to cultivate fear, as patriarchy is about preservation of male property and rights; patriarchal religion codifies those preservation behaviors and consecrates the rights. Males, and the females beholden to them, are trained to perpetually scan for infringements upon those rights.

Threat-scanning is likewise baked into Authoritarian politics, where members are trained to regard outsiders as dangerous by default, and to warily regard those who disagree with or criticize the Authoritarian leader.

Yet Threat-scanning doesn't take hold so well in those who don't have a neurophysiological disposition for it. This leads us to all kinds of odd and interesting variations - the Christian Left, for instance, which embraces Christ not as sword-wielding champion, but as the embodiment of social justice. It leads us to Framer politics, eschewing Authoritarian rule for a system of governance and law that requires openness to opposition. It deflates the cult of personality, which thrives on the comforts of imagined intimacy, intimacy that must be increasingly guarded, however illusory its underpinnings.

In short, the institutionalization of Threat-scanning does us much harm and little good, in the end; and such institutions can never prevail, because they require acquiescence that can never be all-pervasive.

Let the Threat-scanner scan - it's what he was born to do. But don't push him away; that only creates another threat.

(Turn to Page 100)

Common Purpose and Classic Rock

Part of the theory of social cognition that we discuss here at FTW involves the social bonds of prehistoric humans - people who differed (as we do) in our social cognition, for genetic reasons, but who functioned in marvelous cooperation in a dangerous world.

One factor we have isolated that drove this cooperation was common purpose: Homo sapiens lived in a very dangerous world, enduring an ice age while clinging to a precarious link in the food chain. Only through deeply integrated effort and unfailing mutual support did human tribes prevail. And they were bound by the greatest of all natural motivators: the collective drive to survive.

We no longer share that common purpose. We live in a world that is comparatively threat-free, looking back at our ancestors. The odds of any of us starving are vanishingly small; none of us knows anyone who was eaten by a leopard.

But I'm going to argue that 'common purpose' need not be so lofty; there are things that bind us, across sociopolitical boundaries, that are far less weighty than survival, yet create deep harmony and cooperation between those who might be rivals in other contexts.

One of these is music.

I am a member of a classic rock band, playing the music of Boston and Journey and Styx and Kansas and Foreigner et al. Originally, I was just filling in when the previous keyboard player had just gone to jail. I didn't intend to stay long, and in fact the band became (and remains) logistically difficult for me - but I grew to enjoy my bandmates, who are both talented and amiable, and the music has gotten better and better.

Why is he telling us this?

I'm telling you this because, while the band is a democracy, Frank (the lead guitarist) and I are the drivers of change, pushing the band to the next level

- arguing for more difficult (and more revered) songs, a more generalized image, better marketing, better tech support. And Frank and I are as opposite as it is possible to be.

Frank is a hard-right Republican, Trump voter, working man from the manufacturing world; I am way none of that, obviously. Frank believes that the US is doing fine under Trump/GOP rule, and that any words to the contrary are Hillary butt-hurt. Everyone knows what I think.

But Frank and I are as close as can be. We have no interest whatsoever in tearing each other down over those differences. The focus of our friendship is our common purpose: embracing and presenting the music we love so deeply, and the joy of that shared experience on stage.

The point is crystal-clear: if we are able to bond across today's vitriolic boundaries over something as innocuous and inconsequential as "Stone in Love" and "Feels Like the First Time," what other common purposes might we find and build on, to cross our great divide?

Boob Myths

Nature equipped the female primate with the most elegant and ingenious form of fertility regulation: while she is nursing her infant, she does not get pregnant.

It is widely believed that this natural birth control is unreliable, if not outright mythical; and, sure enough, breastfeeding as practiced in Western societies does not prove to be very reliable.

But there's a good reason for that, it turns out: we do it wrong.

How dare you! comes the refrain, who are you to say we do it wrong? Fortunately, this news isn't my own - it comes from Dr. Robert Sapolsky, who has spent a lengthy and fruitful career studying primate behaviors, and the endocrinology of aboriginal humans in particular.

First, a meaningful statistic: while Western women have the experience of only rickety success with breastfeeding as birth suppression, the World Health Organization has global numbers - and estimates that breastfeeding prevents more births annually than all other forms of birth control combined, around the world.

What is the difference, then, between Western breastfeeding and breastfeeding elsewhere in the world?

Per Sapolsky, two factors: frequency and duration. Primates, prehistoric females, and women around the world today who are not subject to the mores of Western society nurse their children far more frequently - as often as every 30 minutes, sometimes. Breastfeeding is accompanied by the release of prolactin, which suppresses ovulation - an effective natural birth control. Steady breastfeeding, even through the night, keeps prolactin levels more or less constant - while feeding a child fewer than 10 times a day, common in Western societies, results in windows of wavering prolactin concentration.

As for duration, Western women tend to wean their children as soon as possible - within a year to 18 months of birth. But in the past and around the world, this isn't the norm; breastfeeding often continues through the first few years of a child's life; and that is easily facilitated, as mother and child are almost never apart - another key difference from Western culture.

This also speaks to the wear-and-tear on the female reproductive system in modern Western life, Sapolsky points out: women who birth and nurse as described above only ovulate a few times every three or four years, throughout their lives - 20 or 30 times, tops - whereas Western women will have 15-20 times that many periods, which is cumulatively very rough on the uterus.

This information isn't very useful, I suppose, from a practical standpoint - our culture, our birthing and nursing practices are what they are. But it's a fascinating window into just how differently we live, compared to our distant ancestors, and gives us insight into how the seemingly small details in those differences have tremendous impact.

To Stand for Science

The great pleasure of the 2017 March for Science was having my youngest daughter there with me. It was her first protest rally, and I'm glad this one was her first: we were surrounded by many hundreds of people whose commitment transcended any one cause, any particular agenda - these were people advocating for reality.

These were people who do not live in echo chambers, people who are willing to let go of one idea in exchange for a better one; people who will not embrace an idea in the first place if it is not solidly supported by evidence and subjected to deep scrutiny; people who have made a life choice not to wallow in the make-believe of this or that social circle, but who have the courage to venture out into reality armed only with reason.

These were people I wanted my daughter to see, people who are not impressed by persons of wealth and power and influence, but who prize the teenage student who chooses to spend her weekends engaged in research over celebrities or tycoons or politicians.

These were people addicted to the real world, people filled with knowledge who yearn for more.

To stand for science is to stand for seeing the world as it truly is, rather than how we wish it was or how the powerful insist it must be;

To stand for science is to place knowledge above emotion, to admit that our feelings are as capable of distorting our place in the world as clarifying it;

To stand for science is to cultivate a willingness to let go of one's own perceptions, to release the impressions of the moment and embrace the more stable foundation of shared observation;

To place science above politics is to reach back to a time when human beings did not traffic in false histories and social illusions in order to manage populations, but simply responded to the world in concert, for their mutual well-being;

To place science above group is to reach forward, creating a new era of equality, opportunity, universal benefit and freedom from the toxic thoughts and practices that contaminate the lives of so many;

To place science above self is to achieve a personal empowerment beyond tribe, beyond religion, beyond ideology, to reconnect with reality and honesty and integrity in ways our social frames do not encourage - and to experience a maturity and renewed view of the world, self, and others that flourishes with infinite possibility and wonder.

All of this, and more, I want for my daughter, my friends, and myself...

Empathy and Common Purpose

There's a Nancy Reagan meme floating around social media. It tells how she was anti-gay until her daughter came out; how she was anti-stem cell until Ronnie came down with Alzheimer's. The meme wraps up with a disparaging comment about how Republicans don't care until it happens to them.

However true that may or may not be, it is certainly true that there are many among us whose empathy remains on the shelf until tragedy or need strikes someone close. This isn't a good thing or a bad thing, just a natural thing: the reservoir of empathy in each of us, while socially cultivated (or not) to some degree, is ultimately a matter of personal genetics. Empathy issues from the insular cortex, which varies from person to person (the insula also regulates the processing of social emotions, plus or minus, and is the center of 'disgust,' shown to be a predictor of sociopolitical bias).

But, consider: however much empathy one might naturally possess, the degree of it we have for others gets activated at the point closest to us - all of humanity, in one extreme, and only our closest family members, in another. How much empathy we muster for others, then, is tied to how much we identify our circumstances with theirs.

What if our circumstances were identical to everyone else's?

In prehistory, we lived and died as one. A human tribe was a united thing, sojourning through territories in collective waves. The people we knew yesterday, today and tomorrow were the same, births and deaths excepted. The point being - those things that happened in the world around us happened to us all.

When our circumstances are the same, when the threats and rewards of life happen to everyone in our world - not just to self or family - then empathy extends to all, whether one naturally possesses a little or a lot. And the sharing of the threats and rewards of life united us in common purpose, fixing our empathy constructively and universally. Unlike our chimpanzee cousins, whose empathy was utterly self-oriented, we took our bonobo-like social sophistication to new heights when we began to wander the world, embracing shared purpose.

United in common purpose - a formula for the emergent flourish of empathy - a world where caring isn't the exception, because what we care about literally applies to all. It's an appealing thought, isn't it?

(Turn to Page 81)

The Eyes Have It

Looking into one another's eyes is a trait that separates two species from all the rest: human beings and our cousins, the bonobos. All the rest focus on head movements and other cues for social communication.

Consider that we and our cousins are, by far, the most social creatures on the earth, and have been for several million years. Consider also that we cannot attribute this great success, leveraging social communication for cooperation and survival, to language - for we have only had language for about 100,000 years, the most recent two percent of our ancestral line's existence.

How were we communicating before then, and how could we have done it so well?

Before anyone says, "Telepathy!", let's hear from Donna Armstrong, a professor of epidemiology, commenting on the pre-linguistic origins of human cooperation:

"Over a period of at least five million years, since the emergence of the hominid line, the capacity evolved for extremely sensitive emotional connecting with other group members. By signaling through fine-tuned muscles of the face and other body language, emotional approval and disapproval could be rapidly and very sensitively conveyed. Our first language - even of contemporary humans - is reading and responding to the unspoken emotional cues and signals of other people. We constantly practice an ancient, highly nuanced body language with each other. We especially read, in each other's faces, extremely rapid, subtle emotional signals, and these emotional experiences are a constant part of our cognitive processing of others and ourselves. Evolutionary selection for size and complexity of the brain system, along with upright stature and other adaptations, supported the development of this emotional experience and primary communication in humans."

Wow.

It only takes a moment's thought to see that communication system still at work, doesn't it? And most of us have noticed that its absence in online digital communication often leads to misunderstanding and social chaos. The take-home point: that we are gifted with the emotional richness of one another's faces makes human communication possible. It is not a gift to be taken for granted. Wise, perhaps, to set words aside, and simply listen by seeing...

"A day may come when these recovered memories may grow as vivid as if we in our own persons had been there and shared the thrill and the fear of those primordial days; a day may come when the great beasts of the past will leap to life again in our imaginations, when we shall walk again in vanished scenes, stretch painted limbs we thought were dust, and feel again the sunshine of a million years ago."

~H.G. Welles, "The Grisly Folk"

Most People

Most people are not greedy - they are content with food, water, shelter, enough to live comfortably.

Most people are not hostile - they are agreeable, enjoy not only their families but their neighbors, are welcoming to those they meet in the street.

Most people are not manipulative - they are happy to be themselves around those they live and work with, and would prefer to trust others, rather than distrust.

Most people are not destructive - they respect what they possess and are happy to respect what others possess.

Most people are loving - they seek to bond with a mate, to nurture their children, and to maintain healthy affection and support for those they hold close.

Most people are content - they care so little about having a vast excess of money and property that they exert only the minimal effort to acquire it.

I say "most" because we all know of exceptions to these claims. But the truth is that these statements define the human norm. We are NOT savage brutes, out to rob and kill one another, held to cooperation only by the threat of law - we are generally peaceful, cooperative creatures innately, and our impressions to the contrary are driven by the high profile of the exceptions.

Can we take this to heart and modify our impressions? Can we arrive at a new and better assessment of human nature? And if so, how can this benefit us?

The Evolution of Trust

Once there was a hormone named oxytocin. It lived within mammals, and functioned to stimulate milk production in females and to trigger infant response through skin contact.

As with most hormones, it found itself repurposed. And, today – along with kissing – it has led to who we are and why we are.

Remember the last time you were naked in your lover's arms, caressing and touching and being inundated with the sensation of well-being? That's oxytocin on the job.

Now, consider: only we can do that.

All mammals mate. Many animals, including mammals, can touch for reasons beyond mating. Some mammals – primates – have hands, rather than paws, and are capable of deliberate touch, and can even hold their young and embrace one another, as we do… Releasing oxytocin, as we do.

But only we can bathe in oxytocin, taking sustained journeys into the delight of extended touch and enhanced pleasure, as we do – because we are relatively hairless, compared to our cousins. Imagine any other creature – *any* other creature! – pulling this off, wrapping limbs around one another, ensnared in passion, rolling lasciviously across a bearskin rug. Dogs? No. Cats? No. Elephants? Pigs? Giraffes?

Stroking a coat of fur does indeed trigger oxytocin release. That's the basis of human pets. Docs and cats and even mice and horses give us their freedom, their loyalty, entering into interspecies bonding because we give them, through petting, greater oxytocin exhilaration than they can achieve with their own kind.

Similarly, touching and caressing are the basis of the social bonds of other primates, despite their fur coats. They touch and caress and build those same bonds, stir that same mutual trust.

Why trust?

It is the basis of oxytocin's most primitive function: breast-latch between mother and infant. This is the most ancient of touch-bonds between mammals, and is more enduring than the other one (genital intercourse).

All other social bonding, all other repurposing of touch and oxytocin, derive from this origin.

Why does our hairlessness put us far out front of all other species, in this regard? Because hair dampens, to some degree, our oxytocin response. Sure, having our hair stroked feels nice, but having our naked flesh stroked feels far, far nicer.

This was a driver in our sexual evolution. Moreover, it was a driver in our social evolution: the consequence of intimate touch is trust, from mother and infant to humans and their pets. In between those two can be found the entirety of all human contact.

As we evolved, we had no taboos or mores to restrict this amazing gift – and, consequently, our social function was staggering. Humans and their predecessors cooperated their way through endless hazards and threats and catastrophes, on the basis of deep and sustained trust, achieved through constant, life-long contact within the clan.

Today, of course, we hardly touch at all. We cooperate well, on a macro level, but struggle with even the most basic relationships on an intimate level. And trust? It is the exception, not the rule.

We can even see, against this evolutionary backdrop, that the surest way to control and manipulate the human mind and heart is to restrict human touch.

And thus we have religion…

The Consequences of Misunderstanding Human Nature

We base our judgments of self and others upon our understanding of human nature, our subjective perception of what a human being is, how we function, how we grow and change. And it is not a surprise to anyone that human beings tend to group themselves according to this particular piece of worldview.

Our assumptions about human nature, however, are almost always (and should be) suspect, for the sources of this viewpoint are likewise suspect. A partial summary of where we get our ideas about human nature include our (equally subjective and tainted) parents and family members, peers, ancient holy books, media, and various educational systems - all of which serve only to perpetuate, and even amplify, existing flaws in our understanding.

The horror of this circumstance is that these competing views of human nature are all necessarily tainted and incorrect, and no sound basis for the establishment of social policy for the common good. No one religion can deliver universal peace and well-being; no one ideology can truly be good for all; no one economic viewpoint can establish a satisfying outcome for all participants. *All* of these systems of thought and behavior are based on specific and subjective (and inflexible) ideas about what a human being really is.

All of this can change, if we agree to rethink our social structures in the light of an objective account of human nature, one that recognizes and addresses the reality of human thought and emotion and group behaviors without the subjective (and often selfish) assumptions of religion and ideology and personal bias. Only one path leads us there - Science - and, well, that's hard work. But hard work should not deter us. We built the pyramids. We landed on the moon. We conquered smallpox and polio. And all of those things were hard. An objective, real account of human nature, free of subjective assumption and emotional shadows, would be a path to growth and universal prosperity unequaled in all of time and history and human thought...

(Turn to Page 103)

Messaging

It is common for religious or political groups, faced with opposition or a lack of member influx, to say, "If only we could get our message out! People just aren't hearing us!"

The belief that The Message Is All, and lack of clarity or distribution the barrier, is a common mistake deriving from a simple source: every such group is inherently and permanently limited, to some degree, by the cognitive style of its members. The message is clear and obvious to those already in the group because it is crafted around their cognitive style. The entire reason such groups form in the first place is that human beings come in many flavors, in terms of how our brains work - there are distinct cognitive types, and some find Idea A attractive while others gravitate to Idea B. Put simply, it's impossible to get everyone on board with any one sociopolitical/religious agenda, no matter how clear or well-distributed the message.

Put even more simply - since our cognitive differences follow from our deep emotional responses (which differ in intensity, person to person), it's as if we have different emotional languages, far below the surface of our thoughts. So we tend to group ourselves with others who have a deep emotional language similar to our own – and we tend not to hear, let alone understand, the subtle language of those who are different.

The only way we can reach a person outside our circle, then, is not to push our message or agenda on them even harder; instead, we need to stop talking, start listening, and learn to hear that deep emotional language that guides their thoughts, words, and feelings...

Coping with Dunbar

Per anthropologist Robin Dunbar, Homo sapiens only has enough cortical brain tissue to cope with about 150 social relationships.

How do we cope with Dunbar's limit? No human brain, now or ever, has been sufficient to adequately cope with the existence of millions of other human beings - and that is the basis of almost all of humankind's social dysfunction. Technology helps, but doesn't cure; we still have the innate impulse to give our empathy, understanding and intimacy to a small group, and to then diminish, in our social brains, everyone else.

Here's a possibility. Since we conserve empathy and understanding by assigning generic, default assumptions (usually demeaning, even inhuman) to Others, we know that such defaults do in fact conserve our social brainpower. So - why not a new default?

Why not a new go-to perception of the stranger on the street, the lady at the checkout, the guy ahead of us in line? Must a default perception be a negative one?

Why not assume to stranger on the street to be a magnificent being, a god, a marvelous instantiation of human goodness? A being from whom we might learn, whose offerings might inspire us to grow – an encounter with a god?

Here are some facts, upon which to build a new one: there is no object in the known universe, as far as we know, more complex than a human brain. Even our technology hasn't come close. The three pound mass of protein in our skulls is astonishing in its intricacy, its variability, its continuity, and its staggering abilities. Nature has produced nothing else that even comes close, and neither have we, for all our industry.

The smallest, most insignificant child among us is heir to far more than you can offer. How does that make you feel?

The smallest, most insignificant child among us is heir to the most astounding phenomenon in all the stars - consciousness. We are the stirring of the awareness of the universe. Even the word "miraculous" does not fully capture all that we are.

Humankind is infinitely precious, infinitely worth preserving. And every living human, regardless of station, is fully representative of that deep worth. Every human being

How is it even possible that we take each other for granted, let alone devalue one another?

Overwhelming Similarity, Mind-Numbing Difference

The brain in your skull that gives rise to the mind that is you is simultaneously incredibly the same as other human brains and incredibly different.

There are roughly 90 billion neurons in all of our heads - astonishingly complex "switches" that have as many as 10,000 "wires" running into every single one - somewhere between 100 quadrillion and a quintillion connections.

We all have the same "pieces" in our brains, arranged in the same way, we all have that many connections - and that similarity is unmatched anywhere else in the history of life.

At the same time, all of those connections - and, more importantly, the strength of each individual connection - differ, person to person. My brain and the brain of my next-door neighbor have more differences than could be recorded in one hundred million books.

Is it any wonder that we all have the ability to live lives that are remarkably similar, sharing the same complexities and highly intricate social and behavioral requirements? At the same time, is it any surprise that we all see the world around us, and others in particular, so differently?

Reconciling this complexity, this overwhelming similarity and mind-numbing difference, is the work of ages; it can't happen overnight, but it inevitably will. It must, if we are ever to take our place among the stars.

This, I suggest, is how we can embrace our social limits, yet transcend them: accept our place in the universe for all that it truly is and can be, and impart the honors of that status on everyone around us...

Authoritarian. Threat-scanning. Uniformity-seeking.

The authoritarian predisposition is a natural feature of human beings. Its evolutionary basis (we think, for now) is rapid group response to imminent threat. The physiology combines limbic impulses (fight or flight) with social processing (grab your spear and do as our leader says), cortical pattern retrieval (together, we will kill this nasty leopard). Some of us are born with high authoritarian predisposition, some with low; a high is good at defending the tribe; a low is good at scouting for food at the boundaries of our territory.

In modern times, the behaviors that follow from the authoritarian predisposition are unfortunate. For a start, authoritarians tend to cluster together - in churches, in political parties - rather than to mingle with the general population. The reason is that such people feel safer when mirrored on all sides by those who take their high levels of fear and discomfort seriously.

A high Threat-Scanning level - a function of the amygdala, the right lobe of which is larger in such individuals - converts this impulse into collective social behavior: wary attitudes toward out-groups, seeing dangers that aren't really there, and so on.

The authoritarian will also tend to have lower levels of empathy - a consequence of a smaller insular cortex (genetically linked) - and thus will have an easier time rejecting out-group members.

Finally, there is sensitivity to Novelty, the opposite of which is an emotional desire for Uniformity. This follows from high levels of dopamine receptors in the authoritarian, meaning that they are rapidly satisfied with "sameness" and disquieted by difference (and also genetically linked).

Put all of these things together, and you have religious extremism, racism - all the social expressions of a group that makes war on other groups, by its very nature.

(Turn to Page 128)

Grandparenting

The joy of knowing one's children's children is not completely unique to modern humans, but it's close. Throughout prehistory - for literally several million years - such a pleasure was unknown to almost all.
Why? Simply put, the average human didn't live long enough to see their children become parents.

Nature gave us every chance. Modern humans delay their offspring's entry into adulthood by 5-10 years, by social design, but in prehistory we began reproducing as soon as our bodies were sexually capable - in our early teens. And with no knowledge of where babies came from, each healthy female would give birth every few years, throughout her life - none lived to reach menopause.

Why did we live such brief lives?

We are now pretty certain it wasn't for lack of the stuff of life. The concept of brutish, harsh existence in our formative years turns out to be mostly comparative projection - we were highly skilled at finding food and water and achieving warmth, even in ice ages.

But we were also cat food - surrounded at all times by species faster and more powerful than ourselves, able to pick us off in a moment of carelessness. Though we became skilled at fighting predators in groups, and frightening them off with fire, the luck of any one individual could only hold out so long.

And like most creatures of the wild, who also seldom die of old age, we were without repair - injury and illness took their toll. Many of the excavated skeletons of our ancestors show multiple instances of damage, and poor healing of each.

With the average lifespan tapering off in the early twenties, individuals lasting long enough to see their own children reproducing - even at 13 or 14 - would have been very rare. Few and far between would have been the moments of bouncing-on-the-knee, the sneaking of candy, the hand-them-back-to-mom-and-dad-when-they-get-surly.

Though 'civilization' drained a great deal away from human social potential, it did impart a gift or two - and longer life stands out as perhaps the greatest of these. Longer life, and longer love...

Adam Smith and Human Nature

He is a god to many in the world of finance, a source of almost holy wisdom when it comes to the perception of capital and wealth and their application to human social organization.

On the one hand, his theories are in line with other big thinkers of the time, and thus has long enjoyed a great deal of academic support; on the other, he wrote a century before we even learned what human beings really are.

Smith's economic theories turn on his understanding, in the middle of the 18th century, of human nature. That makes sense, of course, and his effort was earnest: his *Theory of Moral Sentiments* takes great pains to explicate the nuance and causes of human behavior.

Even so, his perception of human nature was deeply flawed - understandably so, given the limited information available to him: not only do human beings *not* behave as his theories anticipate, not even close; they are predisposed and motivated by forces Smith could never have fathomed - and which few people fully understand, even today.

This being the case, it might be disturbing to some that the human agencies at work in the markets today are operating on such rickety assumptions; and, indeed, there is far too much oscillation in our economies as a result. We know far more today about human behavior and motivations than we knew even 25 years ago, but so deeply ingrained are Smith's thoughts in our economics that a meaningful retooling of market-based economies would be catastrophically disruptive.

And even those 25 years of new perspective on human nature are not needed to know that Smith was off-base. A full seven decades ago, John Nash realized, and then demonstrated, that outcomes are more favorable to collective cooperative behavior than individual competitive behavior (a truth being exploited in the practice of consumer analytics today).Yet another unsettling example of how misunderstanding in the human gestalt can become a danger to human progress...

(Turn to Page 170)

A Cro-Magnon Quartet

Chuck is a young Cro-Magnon in the Middle Paleolithic. An Egalitarian Opportunity-scanning Novelty-seeker, he is a skilled tracker, leading one of his tribe's hunting teams. He is inventive, adept at detecting patterns. He has found that his team performs best when they pool their insights and knowledge of environment, weather, and sign. He performs best, knowing that the portion of the tribe back at camp is safe; as a consequence, he could be called a risk-taker.

Roger is a young Cro-Magnon in Chuck's tribe. He has an Authoritarian Threat-scanning Uniformity-seeker, with no skill for pattern detection but possessed of uncommon diligence and alertness. He works 'third shift,' keeping the basecamp's fire going at night, which provides warmth within and protection from the predators without. He is uninterested in pooled insights or deliberation - he is a man of action. He is more afraid of the dangers around the tribe than most others, but this makes him the ideal security officer.

and introducing...

Jessica is a kinswoman of Chuck and Roger, an Egalitarian Threat-scanning Novelty-seeker. Like Chuck, she is an exceptional pattern-finder, and is skilled at detecting signs in foliage that lead to yummy roots and nutritious caterpillars. Her strong sense of future events leads her to participate in long-term planning, where she is frequently critical of alternatives. She resists the leadership of any one individual while simultaneously remaining wary of too many options.

Betty, another kinswoman, is an Authoritarian Opportunity-scanning Uniformity-seeker, and - like Chuck - a basecamp person. She isn't particularly jumpy about sabertooth tigers, but is worried about eating through the cold season. She is a do-it-yourself person, bored with the yakkity-yak of her peers, and whoa! What do you know? She just invented pottery.

A time warp happens, and...

Chuck, Jessica, Roger and Betty suddenly find themselves in the 21st century.

Chuck is a writer and musician, constantly pursuing his muse, endlessly scouring the world around for inspiration. He loves meeting up with friends to hash out new and different ideas and unusual concepts. A progressive liberal, he favored Hillary in 2016, finding Bernie's campaign style confrontational and unappealing. Though he makes decent money, Chuck doesn't care about money, and hovers on the edge of famine with indifference.

Jessica is a clinical psychologist, doing mostly family work but occasionally called in to consult with tricky cases at the local drug and alcohol treatment center. Likewise a progressive liberal, she has no problem with Bernie's confrontational style, supporting him rabidly and calling for a DNC housecleaning. She serves on the local school board, where she is not well liked.

Roger is a partner in a lucrative insurance firm, a proud Trump voter and a deacon in his church. He is uncomfortable around people he doesn't know, and crunches numbers in his office while others in the firm do the handshaking. He is resentful of his tax bill and wary of his mayor and town council, let alone the parasites in Washington. He believes the US needs a firm hand, and Trump is just the man to provide it.

Betty has a knack for cooking, canning, and candle making, and is pragmatic to the core. Her career as an elementary school teacher leaves her time for all of these things, as her workday ends early. She does not suffer fools gladly, which makes it a good thing she isn't teaching high school. She noisily voted for Gary Johnson, though Jill Stein resonated more deeply with her. She loves the outdoors, and longs to one day own a farm.

The point is openly clear: in the modern world, these four would despise each other; in the distant past, their lives depended on each other. What exactly has changed? The weather and the cat population...

(Turn to Page 200)

Trauma and Attention

Someone I know has suffered severe trauma - emotional trauma, from which the path back can be problematic at best. Her suffering has brought about a shift in worldview, from constant Opportunity-seeking in youth to perpetual Threat-scanning in adulthood.

The source of her trauma was horrific, and need not be detailed here. But the consequence is that her adult life has been a continuing spiral into deeper and deeper paranoia, to the point of delusion.

It's a vicious circle now: the more paranoid she becomes, the more empty the promises and assurances of family, friends and therapists seem; the more empty the assurances seem, the weaker her trust in those around her; the weaker the trust in those around her, the more paranoid she becomes.

This vicious circle is typical in those who have been betrayed by the social universe, exploited or damaged by others in ways that disrupt the already-tenuous social machinery that enables us all. Such people steadily lose their connection to others, leaving them alone, isolated, alienated, terrified. It is easy to characterize this as a living death.

Moreover, there is little to be done, when professional help is eschewed; the only path to connection is to share in the delusion, and to share in it is to feed it, which only makes things worse in the long run.

Why is he telling us this?

I'm telling you this because we've talked about how Threat-scanning, as a component of personal cognition, is by-and-large genetically inherited. But trauma is a singular circumstance: it blows out cognitive circuitry in the brain, blasting away synaptic connections that developed over years in a flash, chunking out connections to the cortex, experience, graduated response. It creates a Threat-scanner where no Threat-scanner was found before, leaving a person in a perpetual state of Threat, doing nothing but scanning for new dangers, all of them imagined.

And where Threat reigns, Attention is truncated, hyper-focused on imaginary demons. The benefits of reflection, deliberation, and contemplation - cortical blessings - all fade into uselessness. These benefits are respite to those whose limbic and cortical activity are balanced; in the traumatized, they are all but gone.

There is no easy answer. There is little we can do but watch someone we love suffer endlessly. All that remains is compassion...

Binary Thinking

When we feel threatened, our attention narrows to focus on whatever is threatening us. This is an ancient gift of evolution, and is has a downside: it kicks in regardless of whether the threat is real or imagined, physical or abstract. Words, for instance, can cause us to tighten up inside as if a big dog were leaping at us. And as attention narrows, the breadth of thought we have available for decision narrows with it. Rapid response to threat is generally limbic response - a fast impulse to act or not act, to leap left or leap right. Our thinking becomes binary - *this!* or *that!* – not really 'thought' at all. It's pure reaction.

Put another way, our threat-scanning tendencies erode our quality of evaluation and decision. More often or not, such dichotomies are utterly false. Since our threat-scanning tendencies operate even in social domains where they aren't even needed, we often find ourselves truncating our thinking over matters which absolutely deserve our thorough deliberation – response, rather than reaction.

Binary thinking also serves another easily misaligned purpose: it simplifies things. If, in making a decision, we only allow ourselves to see two options, decision comes more easily. This, too, is evolution's gift: our brains are packed to bursting with shortcuts that simplify the world, and this is one of them. But we often have the luxury of time, in our comfy present day. We can, most of the time, find a third option, and a fourth, and realize that the choices we are faced with aren't always *this* or *that*, but sometimes *this* *and* *that*, *or* possibly *those*.

Finally, we have cause to be wary. Our leaders, our religions, our various in-groups often present us with false binary choices, in an effort to steer our thinking and pull our strings. They load us up with *this* good, and *that* is evil. *This* is what you can choose, and *that* is what we cannot accept, if you want to be one of us…

The easiest out, when we're faced with opposition, is binary opposition: if you're not *with* me, you're my *enemy*! There are only two sides, mine and *not* mine! But, of course, the world isn't that simple: *My* way vs. Your Way vs. All the Other Options is a labyrinth of potential directions…

Binary This/That is a technique as old as the hills, and it often works. But the closest any leader or group can get to our individual capacity to evaluate and decide and act is the words they use to put a threat or decision in front of us.

The binary thinker, in our private social circle or in public office, cannot see our cognitive struggle, our wrestling to reconcile what seems right within to what seems right by the cries of those around us.

The binary thinker is insensitive to the nuance of rightness among the wide range of best outcomes for the masses, the subtleties of *This Works!*between those of us who are not like most people.

Whether we react to it or response to it is ultimately up to us.

"I say in speeches that a plausible mission of artists is to make people appreciate being alive at least a little bit. I am then asked if I know of any artists who pulled that off. I reply, 'The Beatles did.'"

~Kurt Vonnegut

Human Brains and the World As It Is

"We don't see things as they are; we see them as we are." ~Anaïs Nin, H. M. Tomlinson, Steven Covey, et al

Every human brain is unique; every human brain has its own distinct features. And every human brain is inherently limited.

Because our worldview and ability to cooperate (or not) with others derive from the features of our brains, and because these features differ, one person to another, no one person can achieve an objective, absolute worldview. Something in the way each of us perceives the world and other people will always be missing. No one truly sees the world as it is.

It is even correct to say that part of the point of the human brain, and the social brain in particular, is to filter reality. Any mind that took in and processed absolutely everything the world presented to it would necessarily be vast, not simply huge but far more complex than even the very-complex brains nature has bestowed upon us. The ability of the brain to simplify, categorize and prioritize is less a weakness than a blessing.

All the same, one of our most insidious mental toxins is the conviction that this filtering can deliver any absolute truths, the illusion that How We See It Is How It Is. This belief, nestled in one mind or many, becomes a bludgeon: 'If what I see is real, then what you see must not be.' Countless are those who have met their doom for the sin of cognitive difference, falling to the swords of holy war, the fires of inquisition or the conceits of manifest destinies.

Those impulses still reign, as this group or that goes on insisting it must rule all the others from the pinnacle of its self-exalted worldview. But we can look inside human brains now, even watch them at work: we know better. We also know, based on our decades of study of human behavior, that our inevitable differences are necessary to human survival.

What is needed is some mechanism, some socio-intellectual framework that can get us past our innate subjectivity – some way that we can get closer, individually and collectively, to seeing the world as it really is – some means of absorbing the whole of reality, despite the fact that no one of us can get there alone.

How would that work?

The surrender of subjectivity would require that any seeker of knowledge wishing to make a new contribution to the human accumulation must subject it to vigorous attempts at self-refutation – a best-possible effort to disprove the new item; failure to self-refute would be a hard requirement for advancement.

Moreover, the contributor would have to make a best-possible effort to disconnect emotionally from the discovery – to discount their own feeling of "rightness" about the new item.

Since, best efforts aside, it is not possible for any one person to achieve such things completely, the contributor would have to submit the discovery to a company of peers, as knowledgeable or more, its task being to achieve the refutation the contributor could not; only in the case of collective failure to refute would the new item be considered bona fide knowledge.

Furthermore, it would be understood that any such contribution could never be more than tentative, as this new system of discovery – being no respecter of persons – would invite the overturning or revision of *any* knowledge, at any time, regardless of its level of general acceptance or the social status of the contributor, provided the revision passes the test above.

Within such a system, knowledge itself would be the seat of authority, a seat that no one person could seize and hold.

Such a system could never succeed, of course. It would mean a steady ascent to the end of human labor; the conquest of disease; the lengthening of human life; the cessation of the need for market economies; the redistribution of energy – an ending of all enterprises that permit men to dominate one another.

Such a system could never succeed, because it would fly in the face of religions, ideologies, social dominance and other emotional comforts; it would threaten the powerful, invite accusations of heresy and sedition upon its practitioners, and slowly erode even the most entrenched fantasies of modern humans – who, after several thousand years of living in detachment from the world that gave them life – embrace a residual dread that goes unconfronted.But dare to dream...

The Lonely Center

As the US political/religious Right has dragged the nation relentlessly in its own direction over the past three decades, the response of those outside the Right has been two-fold: politicians have generally grown more centrist, and non-politicians (the grass roots and the activists) have begun tugging hard Left.

This tension has begun rending the Left in the same way the Right has been fractured by the tension between its traditionalists and its extremists.

As Democratic centrists have been increasingly cast as stooges for lobbyists and Democratic progressives have become war-whooping revolutionaries, the two groups have managed to not only to reduce their party to levels of disunity comparable to their GOP doppelgängers; they have actually begun generating their own wedge issues. Suddenly where I stand on single payer healthcare defines my political identity more than my position on distributed government.

For awhile there, in the Sixties and Seventies, the Left managed to step beyond the ceaseless pillow-fighting that had come to define party politics in the twentieth century, the constant parading of "moral stance" on issues as the substance of political thought and identity. There was a brief renaissance, a fleeting genuflection to the Founders' intent, as the deliberative functionality of representative government held sway over party aggressions. It didn't last long, but it was enough to remind the children of the children of the great wars that there's more to our form of government than posturing. The Democratic Party had something to do with that, and can be a bit proud of it.

Four decades later, its soul is in the same peril as that of its elephantine cousin: the pillow fights are becoming lead pipe rumbles, and the very structure and process of government are at risk. As Mitch McConnell dismantles the Senate as we've known it, as the Supreme Court becomes a partisan battering ram and the White House itself a wrecking ball, both Left and Right may soon lose their very capacity for cooperation in government, will and intentions aside.

Before that happens, the Left needs to take stock: if it all continues to be about issues, if the path to governance is nothing more than clubbing each other with policy positions, then the existing fractures both within and between parties can only widen; if the structure and process of deliberative policy-making and partisan compromise are not preserved, then the US truly ceases to be a democracy.

To get there, both Left-left and Left-center need to end their respective bids to become the soul of the party. That soul needs to stop being about an issues portfolio and become a way of thinking, a return to inclusion and middle ground. Progressives need to stop howling that *they* are the answer, and the mainstream liberals and moderates need to reach out to moderates and mainstreamers in general - grow their numbers, and grow them not around these or those issues, but around a new way of thinking.

That new way of thinking, of course, isn't new at all - it's the core of the concept of the United States, that citizens can maintain their own governance through adherence to cooperative, deliberative representation - and we know that this principle is older still, a return to the cooperation and social cohesion that defined human community before the dawn of civilization. It's the idea that we all need one another to survive - that autonomy is a lie, that My Ideas and My Group are not the end-all, be-all, but that we are stronger and more successful when everyone's contribution matters. That idea has carried not just the US but humankind as a whole through far more than tumultuous political cycles - it has carried us through the eons.

Strict Fathers, Nurturant Parents, Explicable Voters

Professor George Lakoff, cognitive scientist and linguistics expert at Berkeley, has some thoughts about modern politics, and the inexplicable behaviors of partisan voters in particular. He shares two models that make these behaviors clear.

Voting, he argues, is based on our innate responses to authority – and these are learned in childhood, he points out.

The Strict Father

"About 35 percent of Americans have what I call 'Strict Father morality'," Lakoff said in an interview on the *Make Me Smart* podcast. "That is, they believe that "father knows best," that father is the authority, that what he says is right, that if children don't obey him, they have to be given tough love and punished until they do – and that this gives rise to a view that you have to be disciplined."

Within this frame, parental authority is just that – authoritarian. The edict of the father is all, and forms the basis of acquiescence to one's social group, one's sociopolitical bias, and in the case of patriarchal religion, one's role in spiritual community.

In his book *Don't Think of an Elephant!*, which is a primer on the framing of political rhetoric, Lakoff points to Evangelical icon James Dobson, of "Focus on the Family" fame, who advocates a particularly harsh agenda for the parenting of very small children, as an example of Strict Father morality and how it works. Human beings are born selfish, in this frame, and must have cooperation and obedience instilled in them through perpetual physical discipline. Lakoff's point is that this mindset remains, long after early childhood has passed.

The Strict Father frame then becomes all-pervasive in the minds of its adherents, Lakoff said, generating a universal hierarchy.

"You have God above Man - we've conquered nature, you have Man above Nature, we can take anything we want for our use – you have the strong above the weak – that hierarchy follows, from one idea… it's Strict Father Morality applied to all aspects of life."

And this explains Donald Trump, whose victory in 2016 was inexplicable – but no so much as the unwavering support from his conservative, Evangelical base, who continued to support him despite his complete lack of conservative bona fides and his clear commitment to hedonism.

"[Strict Father morality] is what Trump not only believes, but acts on and assumes is correct – and he knows that about 35 percent of the country, the 35 percent who still support him also believe this, even if they're poor. The main thing is, if that is your worldview, and that's your morality, that defines who you are as a person; it's self-definition. And people don't vote against their self-definition. Not only that, it doesn't matter if Trump lies to them, and they know he's lying, because there's a higher truth – which is Strict Father Morality *itself*, which has consequences, and they are truer than any lies – and that if you deny that, if you accept the lies as more important, you're denying your self-identity. That's why there are 'alternative facts'."

The Nurturant Parent

Strict Father Morality is not the end of the story, per Lakoff: There is another parenting style at the other end of the frame, where Mom and Dad are equals, and the upbringing of a child is more a matter of nurture and encouragement than correction and discipline. And this frame also forms the basis of sociopolitical bias and adult moral impetus.

"[This] is what I call 'nurturant morality'," Lakoff said. "That is, you care about other people. In the family, adults care about their children, are honest with them, they try to talk directly with them and have an answer to all their questions, they take care of them and they want them to be fulfilled in life, and they want them to care about other people. And that comes out as a progressive moral view, which goes like this: that citizens care about other citizens, work through the government to provide public resources for everybody, starting with business – you can't have a business if you don't have streets and roads and airports and sewers and science…and that isn't the government, it's the people, the public - the private depends on the public. If you have Strict Father Morality, then you did it all, it's personal responsibility."

Lakoff's ultimate point is devastatingly clear: the Strict Father frame and the Nurturant Parent frame define the politics of our time – and historically, all times – and explain our political and social divides perfectly, while also lending insight into the underlying psychology of our personal worldviews.

Lakoff extends his ideas by pointing out that all voters have at least an innate understanding of both frames, if committing to only one, and that both frames may be activated by language – and this explains the relative success or failure of political rhetoric around us. Greater balance may be achieved in our political discourse, he argues, if all voters can become more aware of political frames and more critical of the rhetoric.

Finally, Lakoff's Strict Father/Nurturant Parent model syncs up nicely with Altemeyer's model of Authoritarianism and the cognitive types of sociopolitical bias: leader-vs-group, threat-vs-opportunity, change-vs-not. It infuses our understanding of irreconcilable worldviews and divisive rhetoric with a renewed sense of possibilities and high utility.

(Turn to Page 188)

A Town Where Ducks Lived

Soren Kierkegaard, the Danish philosopher-theologian, tells the story of a town where ducks lived.

The ducks would wake up in the morning and leave their duck homes and go out into the duck streets to the duck Wal-Mart or the duck McDonald's, going about their duck business. And on Sunday they would all gather in the duck church, and the duck minister would stand in the duck pulpit and open the duck bible and say, "Ducks! God has given us wings! We can mount up as eagles and soar, no longer confined to the mundane existence of waddling!"

And all the ducks cried, "Amen!" ...and they all waddled home.

Kierkegaard is being critical of the church, obviously, making the point that religious faith is more often than not a case of potential not even pursued, let alone achieved.

I want to argue that it's that way beyond the domain of religion, too.

We live in a culture that is anti-intellectual, to say the least, where skepticism and critical thinking are not only not encouraged, but held in disdain. And I suggest that this is flat-out criminal.

Even people of modest intelligence have enormous potential for improved quality of thought and understanding. The human capacity for strong perception and good reasoning are formidable, even when unremarkable. Why, then, do we not do a better job of it?

1. We are never taught to do so. Critical thinking and reasoning, and a skeptical perspective regarding new information, are not priorities anywhere but in scientific training. Our schools do not place a premium on them.

2. The rewards of critical thinking and thoughtful deliberation are slow in coming. There is little or no immediate gratification in taking the time to

ponder new information or complex decisions; we actually have to seek out the rewards for these efforts, they do not present themselves overtly.

3. People who think critically and understand deeply are very hard to control, and there are many out in the world - in positions of leadership, particularly - who stand to lose when facing a population of strong and perceptive thinkers.

On the other side of it, however, consider this:

1. Critical thinking and expanded understanding and perception are achievable by anyone, for free. Anyone can pursue these things, simply by mustering the will to do so.

2. The rewards of deeper thought and understanding, while abstract, are ours to define. Achievements like these mean something different to each of us, and can become sources of satisfaction that we can shape as we wish.

3. If we are harder for others to control and manipulate, then we are more independent, more free to pursue our own course. This, more than any other reason, makes taking flight worthy of the challenges and risks.

On Fairness

Primates are the most social creatures on earth. We have a strong sense of one another and are capable of complex perceptions and interactions. And one principle we are capable of enacting through individual choice is to exchange our submission to social existence for fair treatment from the group.

Frans de Waal has a Ted Talk on YouTube that gives a humorous but poignant illustration of our sensitivity to unfair treatment, even in our smallest and most distant cousins (we are divided from monkeys by more than 30 million years at this point). Two Chapuchin monkeys, side by side in cages, are given a task: accept a rock handed to them by a lab assistant and put it on a shelf. Their reward: a slice of cucumber – acceptable but not lavish, as rewards go. The first monkey executes the task and accepts the cucumber. The second monkey executes the task, but then is given a big, juicy grape as a reward, as the first monkey looks on. The first monkey is given another rock, and is rewarded with another piece of cucumber. He throws it back angrily at the lab assistant – rejecting it, though it was perfectly acceptable the first time around, because it is unfair. The scene is hilarious, but also very telling.

"This is basically the Wall Street protest that you see here," quips de Waal in the video.

Fairness is the glue that holds our species together. Our hundreds of thousands of years of survival against all odds occurred because the rewards of that survival went to every member of the group. There was no inequality, no hierarchy, no domination of some by others.

Our social cooperation is life-or-death for our species. Some sociopolitical orientations are built around "Every man for himself!" - others say the opposite. Some say "Each according to his contribution," and then define "contribution" very conveniently for themselves. Some say "Each according to his need," with no concern for contribution. We see these orientations in data gathered on moral values claims ("Fairness" is one of five key moral values measured), then correlated with self-reported political affiliation.

The point being, we vary greatly in our sensitivity to fairness, and our sense of obligation to provide it. It is telling that those who, by their own claim, place the least moral value on fairness are those who, demographically, have the most...

"If man is to survive, he will have learned to take a delight in the essential differences between men and between cultures. He will learn that differences in ideas and attitudes are a delight, part of life's exciting variety, not something to fear."

~Gene Roddenberry

The World in Our Dreams

The causes and functions of dreams have long been debated. We posit that dreaming is the brain's world-modeling capacity in idle, running because the brain seldom goes completely to sleep; dreaming keeps synaptic stimulation in play, which is good for our neurons, while our blood cleanses them after a long day.

Last night I had an unusual variation on a decades-long dream. The dream's origins are of a three-story house, broken into student apartments, in Lexington, south of UK. I never lived there - no such building ever existed - but I have dreamed of that building dozens of times over the years. In the dream, the building is a labyrinth, and my second-floor flat is connected to other areas in all sorts of ways. I am also afraid to go there, because I have rented it in defiance of my parents.

Make of that what you will, last night I returned, and the building was now vast - basically three huge, multilevel buildings, all interconnected. And I spent much time there.

Here's the thing: the layout of the building was utterly improvised. I have never been in such a building in my life: it contained components one never finds in a single building, from a library to a nursery to a cube farm to a newsroom to a wading pool.

I made several circuits of the building, and the layout - completely invented in my subconscious and presented to me in the dream - remained consistent. Little details were so vivid and accurate that I went into waking-dream mode and realized I was dreaming, surprised at the dream's fine resolution, even as I walked thru the newsroom and saw a copy of the APA stylebook on a desk next to an IBM Selectric. The nursery was fully equipped, and I remember sushing myself when I stumbled into it, like Ripley in the queen's hive, so as not to wake any of the infants.

Why am I telling you this? Because Paleolithic humans had the same brains we do, and would have dreamed as we do. They would have built, consciously or subconsciously, variations on the world they knew inside their minds, rich with real-world details deeply ingrained, studying the variations for information and meaning – but ultimately at the mercy of their imaginations.

And here's the thing: their cognitive control over that process would have been deeply limited - seldom can we *make* things happen in our dream – how many times have your dreams of sex remained unconsummated? - and often our dreams completely surprise us, serving up details and twists that sometimes even shock us.

The kicker: as conscious beings, we don't actually live in the real world - we live in the *model* of the real world that exists in our heads. And we can see, with just a bit of study and introspection, that such worlds are not really of our own conscious making. We are, in the end, guided by random subconscious suggestions that have little to do with those things we consciously desire. If all of this is true, we are living well below our potential...

Going Vulcan

Let's address the outpouring of rancor and disdain from Left to Right that has not only been unceasing but increasing, since the 2016 presidential election.

Most of it is directed at the White House and the GOP that cowers behind it, of course, but there is plenty to go around, and Right-wing media outlets and talking heads are garnering no small share. There's motivation a-plenty for this outpouring: much of it derives from growing trepidation (and even outright fear); a great deal is blossoming from easily-justified moral indignation.

But I want to suggest that it might be a good idea to take the rancor and disdain and dial them down about six notches. As understandable as they are, they are not the best response available to us.

We look at Trump and see an unbridled narcissist; we look at the GOP and see craven opportunists embracing Authoritarianism as a matter of utility and convenience; we even wonder if we've spotted a sociopath or two among them.

It's not that what we're seeing isn't real. It is the nature of persons with such behaviors to parade them, so there's not a lot of room for interpretation. Instead, I'm suggesting that our emotional responses to them are not particularly appropriate, let alone useful. Consider these three points...

- We are all of us, every one, socially crippled to some degree. Humankind as a species now lives within a social universe that pushes every single one of us far beyond our social bandwidth - our brains simply don't have the resources to cope, and thus we have taken on countless diminished behaviors and beliefs about others, all misguided, simply for the relief from the cognitive pressure we all endure. By this, I'm saying that *everyone*, not just Donald Trump, started out broken.

- The Non-Authoritarian views the Authoritarian with contempt, by default, but we've already pointed out that the Authoritarian was *born* an Authoritarian - that his cognitive and behavioral predispositions are a product of his individual brain features and personal neurochemistry. This doesn't explain everything, but it does call us to err on the side of tolerance in judging him. The painful step is next: realizing that both the narcissist and the sociopath are *also* born with those predispositions, usually socially stoked in childhood, but enabled by brain features all the same (empathy issues from a portion of the brain where the amount of tissue we each are born with is variable). We should no more despise the narcissist for his behaviors than we should despise an epileptic for convulsing. (It is another thing, of course, to despise the behavior, and to refuse to indulge it; but that is not the same as despising the person, and we are both intelligent and well-educated enough to embrace the distinction.)

- We are narrowing our own attention and social brainpower when we entertain the rancor and disdain. We've discussed how negative emotion pushes us limbic, away from our cortical resources, our powers of reason and understanding. The messes we see growing around us naturally provoke our emotional responses, yes, but we need our reason and understanding more than ever: letting our attention be truncated now by fear and anger, when we need them most, is not in anyone's best interests.

So I'm suggesting we Go Vulcan. We should continue paying close attention to the disturbing march of events, and remain deeply engaged - but the anger and the lashing out are ill-advised. We do ourselves and everyone around us a considerable service when we reign them in...

Authoritarians and US Government

When Dick Armey and Tom DeLay began openly parading their intention to construct a "permanent majority" in the US, effective one-party rule, 12 years ago, the foolishness of such an agenda was clear not only to my progressive friends but my conservative friends, as well - the 2006 Dem sweep of Congress seemed almost a deliberate repudiation of such a position.

Then came the great gerrymander of 2010, and it became clear that the GOP was serious - its desire is to establish itself as permanently in charge.

At face value, this is a threatening circumstance, but it's also perfectly understandable, in the context of the cognitive theory we frequently discuss.

What kind of leadership would an Authoritarian follower crave?

What kind of government would make an Authoritarian follower feel secure?

What kind of role would an Authoritarian follower want government to play in his life?

Now...

What kind of leadership does our constitution provide for? Where does security reside, within that framework? And what is the role of government, per the constitution?

Put simply, the Authoritarian follower's sociopolitical frame - which they come by honestly, as a result of genetics and cognitive clustering - is never likely to feel secure and settled within the social ecosphere of US government. The Framers did not build the US in such a way as to accommodate any one cognitive type, but as a gathering place for all cognitive types (and they did it intuitively, since only Jefferson and Franklin would be likely to even grasp the dynamics of 'cognitive type'). The

Authoritarian follower's emotional predispositions, where social authority and threat are concerned, will not respond well to a political process that denies even superficial satisfactions to his type.

No wonder they would rather see our political landscape collapse in favor of an Authoritarian rule. It would make them feel better, much safer, much more 'normal' - normal for their cognitive type.

We absolutely can't let that happen. But we can stop loathing and despising them for feeling as they do.

(Turn to Page 180)

A Choice of Christs

Secular humanists and liberals take offense at the aggressive, un-inclusive behaviors of many Evangelical Christians, even equating their hostility and bigotry to that of the Taliban.

Evangelical Christians take deep offense to the suggestion that they are anything at all like Muslim extremists.

Both are correct to feel as they do, and both are wrong - and this leads to a breakdown in understanding in dialog that really needs repair.

We know that human beings, from the standpoint of social thinking and understanding, come in several flavors - from the extremely aggressive to the extremely passive, from risk-averse to highly exploratory, from highly defensive to highly empathetic. This diverse mix enabled humankind to survive for hundreds of thousands of years.

That diversity is reflected in the textual portrait of the Christ. Put simply, many Christs can be found in the gospel accounts. And people tend to see the one who reminds them most of themselves.

It could be argued that this is by design - that the Nicean committee that cherry-picked the text we now read in the canonized books intentionally introduced that variety, to attract cognitive types from all over. This is giving them far too much credit, I think - I can't imagine 4th century Romans understanding cognitive type differentiation and still managing to allow their empire to collapse - but even if it were true, we are faced the fact that many of these Christs are emotionally incompatible with one another.

We can see this in the Sermon on the Mount alone. The text, of which even Carl Sagan said (through Eleanor Arroway), "I think the Sermon on the Mount is one of the greatest ethical statements and one of the best speeches in history", is a humanist manifesto, advocating for empathy and unbridled reciprocal altruism, and a blistering admonition of ethnocentrism. It is a clarion call for social justice, a progressive liberal's dream come true.

Simultaneously, it advocates authoritarianism, and in particular authoritarian constrains that explicitly undo all of the above.

Those who choose, where it comes to Christ, are choosing their own cognitive type - which means they really aren't choosing anything at all.

Back to Evangelicals and the Taliban. Many (but certainly not all) conservatives are authoritarian, threat-scanning and uniformity-seeking individuals (call them ATUs). This is who they were born to be, and all of these traits can have strong and positive impact in human groups. It is also true that many Muslims have these traits. And extremists on both sides certainly possess them (including Christians terrorists, such as the KKK, who get to claim the label of 'Christian,' whether non-violent Evangelicals like it or not.

But above our cognitive predispositions, ATU or otherwise, there is a broad behavioral expanse - our tendencies in thought and behavior can lead to an extremely broad range of possible social expressions, from the most violent and abhorrent to the most benign and constructive.

Non-ATU personalities, liberal or no, look at Evangelicals and Taliban and see ATU, and there's some validity to that; Evangelicals look at themselves and at the Taliban and KKK, and see a broad range of behavioral expressions - and there's some validity to that, too.

We need to look deeper into ourselves and into one another - and into the complex nature of the Christ presented in text, for sure...

(Turn to Page 134)

Our Best Selves

Human minds vary in our degree of empathy.

We vary in our degree of aversion to risk. We vary in our interest in the new and unexpected, in our desire for continuity.

We vary in our need for safety, loyalty to our group, and in our comfort with kin; in our levels of compassion, and in the discomfort of vulnerability.

We tend to consider our own levels of such feelings to be 'normal', and to consider differing levels in others to be either insufficiency of character, moral weakness or immaturity.

But this turns out not to be the case. Our variability in our responses to the world, to our environment and each other, makes us stronger as a whole. The problem is, the strengthening of the group through wide variability in social cognition was an adaptation made by relatively small human groups; in the modern world, when we see a thousand people a day, we tend to be less socially aware and less invested in being our best selves for others in the world – because we don't know everyone as intimately as we did in the Paleolithic.

Our challenge is this: how do we self-examine in such a way as to not only bring about our best selves, but the version of ourselves that best serves others, in our modern, complicated world?

It can only be by assessing our personal levels of the traits mentioned above - which are comfortable to us, personally - and asking, Is my current level of empathy/risk-taking/loyalty/compassion/vulnerability making me the best I can be - and if not, what needs changing?

The conservative may self-examine and ask, Am I truly less empathetic and compassion than I might be, as my liberal friend suggests? And the liberal may self-examine and ask, Am I truly reckless, too impulsive, as my conservative friend suggests? The answers would be not only revealing, but constructive - and ultimately, hopefully, bridge-building.

Since our expression of each of these traits comes to us naturally, increasing or decreasing them can only occur with conscious, sustained effort. Human minds can change, but we know that it doesn't happen easily. It only happens when we're deeply committed to the change.

(Turn to Page 140)

The In Crowd

If we have any hope of moving forward as a nation - or, for that matter, if Christian churches wish to have any hope of escaping the negative associations brought upon them by their current political stances - we must put the lie to the legitimacy of cognitive clustering.

We've presented a model for the individuation of thought and emotion underlying social bias (social bias, in turn, underlies political bias), in which human beings, now numbering in excess of our person-by-person ability to fully cope with an excess of social emotion in their world, huddle together in groups who make very, very few demands of them.

We've called this *cognitive clustering*. It is a subconscious survival strategy for coping with so many people in our world - our brains, due to their size and limited prefrontal cortical tissue, can only process the behaviors of about 150 people (Dunbar's limit, which we've discussed). But we are presented with far more, and our brains simply can't do it; it's like trying to run Windows 7 on an 8086 PC.

So we come up with shortcut strategies. One is to 'dehumanize' those outside our group - people of other cultures, skin color, etc - to minimize the number of people we actually deal with as people, even to the point of inventing reasons to exclude them (religion, sexual orientation, gender). Another strategy is cognitive clustering.

Impossible in prehistoric times, because human tribes were so comparatively small, cognitive clustering is the social grouping of persons who have the same or similar cognitive type - neurological predisposition to the same subconscious emotional responses. This works *wonderfully* - it takes little or no effort to socially process the behaviors and words of people who are not only extremely familiar, but extremely similar to ourselves. Put simply, it isn't that much work to go to church and be around people who believe the same things, possess the same biases, and vote the same way.

The real catch here is that we disguise our cognitive clusters in all sorts of ways: we layer religions on top of them; political parties; civic agendas, any and every excuse we can contrive, in order to huddle together with the like-minded.

But no matter our rationale, it just doesn't work: cognitive clustering relieves our individual stress at being around too many people, but as a social fix, it is disastrous; it robs the individual of the experience necessary to be a true cooperator and collaborator, with the proficiency we are all heirs to; it robs the group of the diversity and intellectual dexterity to muster the collective skill it requires to be robust and effective.

Now we get down to it: the anti-Trumps and non-Evangelicals who rail against the Evangelical Trump voters are completely missing what's going on. Evangelicals are not "the Christian Taliban"; they are cognitive clusters of people who happen to have overlapping cognitive type with foreign groups we can safety call terrible people. They didn't choose their cognitive type, they were born with it, and they certainly do not choose beheading as a political option.

The same is true for Trump voters: we are seeing cognitive clusters of people with a certain cognitive type, not fascists; they have grouped together not to make others suffer or to give fealty to the destruction of their government; they are simply gathering together with others who reflect their own cognitive processing - which, again, they did not choose for themselves.

We don't gather into these groups for the "official" reasons we always claim. Few of us truly believe what we claim to believe, in order to justify our group memberships and acceptance - they are the price of admission to the room where we feel most like ourselves.

It is madness to rail at them, because their true commitment is to the safe place that cognitive clustering provides. And it is, moreover hypocrisy: every single person doing the railing is *also* a member of one or more cognitive clusters.

Again, we did not suffer these social cripplings in prehistory, because our numbers were too small for clustering to be possible, let alone necessary. They are a destructive aberration.

Even so, we sure as hell suffer from them now, and there is only one cure: to break up our clusters; to allow those who think differently into our circles; to do the (very) hard and (very) necessary work of endeavoring to understand them, allow for and even appreciate the differences, and (hardest of all) to shut down the horrific judgmentalism and disdain we heap upon them.

Then, and only then, will we be behaving as real human beings, and living up to the high-sounding ideals of the cognitive clusters that divide us...

(Turn to Page 159)

"I like the dreams of the future better than the history of the past."

~Thomas Jefferson

The Redistribution of Attention

Human attention is a much bigger subject of study than you might guess. There are social psychologists, clinical psychologists, and neuropsychologists who make it their entire life's work. There is social attention, sensory perception, child/infant attention - many different sub-branches to this subject.

Our interest here in social attention has probably been understated in our academically-flavored posts. We've talked about how the narrowing of attention as a reflexive response to threat is a natural and hereditary mammalian trait, survival-critical - and we've talked about how this impulse can be redirected in our social group interactions, manipulatively, to truncate critical thinking and deliberative reflection in favor of uglier default reactions.

As above, much study can be made of this dynamic. Those social leaders/groups that seek to control us (political leaders, religious leaders, both in-group and out-group members, the media, businesses trying to sell us things, family members) most often do so through distraction, diversion, triggering on many levels, robbing us of the one thing that we can use to craft the most appropriate and self-/group-healthy response: Attention.

At its core, attention is very simple, and it evolved to work very efficiently. Our early survival depended upon two levels of attention: personal attention to self, solitary task, and environment; and social attention to group signals and shared tasks. Within these two levels, attention is directed and redirected by a number of factors, all of which were consistent among us, modulated only by our individual brain differences and the quality of our social experience.

Today it's not that simple. We are bludgeoned with well-crafted assaults on our attention, for a broad range of purposes - some of them for the greater good, some to exploit us, some to keep us from seeing what someone doesn't want us to see. Most of these assaults negatively affect the quality of our experience with others, and more than a few are direct assaults on our well-being.

What can be done? Step One must be the cultivation of personal awareness - a mindfulness of where our attention is going at any given moment, and a process of determining how and why. Step Two has got to be greater and more focused attention on those who interact with us - a deeper mindfulness regarding our relationships, both intimate and casual. Step Three would be a constant conscious parsing of the messages bombarding us from the social universe, again asking How and Why, without ceasing.

In the end, we reclaim our attention - and it's my guess that achieving that recovery would be an eye-opener: empowering, certainly, because we could not help but realize what we've been missing all this time...

The Sick, the Weak, and the Old

As if it weren't already overexposed, the ugliness of the GOP psyche is more clear today than ever, after the American Health Care Act debacle. As the nation shrieks its disapproval, as every major medical association withholds its endorsement, as GOP aye-voters parade their reluctance, and as the economy braces for impact, we are left wondering - is the relatively small far-right Evangelical base *really* this powerful, *really* this worthy of such pandering?

Or is it something else?

The US is the only first-world nation that continues to cling to the idea that its citizens' health is best left in the hands of capitalism: we aren't even in the Top 30 - all of those "socialist" countries provide their people with better care at lower cost, resulting in higher life expectancies and lower infant mortality.

Is it because, as conservative economics declare, the free market is the place where the best decisions emerge? Obviously not; the pre-ACA system was a shambles, tumbling in the same direction the GOP again wants to take us - healthcare that favors the wealthy and pushes down on the sick and the old.

Is it because capitalism is inherently corrupt, and will put profit above people? We need look back no further than 2008 to be reminded of where unfettered capitalism takes us, but it can't be that simple: unlike the financial industry, which is mostly made of fairy dust, the healthcare industry has no prospect of rebounding without consequence if the system does in fact crash.

Is it because politicians are in the pockets of the major healthcare providers? Again, too simple: while the healthcare lobby is astonishingly powerful, and undoubtedly owns more than its share of congresspeople, many in the GOP's own ranks openly bemoan the cruelty of its party's attitude toward healthcare.

There is something deeper at work.

I suggest that this is very much a moral question. Cruel, the GOP's view of the citizenry certainly is, and the mistake is to view that cruelty in isolation from its roots. It is better to set aside our revulsion at the GOP's apparent inhumanity, and examine what's really going on under the surface.

Our moral impulses do not derive from reason, nor do they emerge from contemplation, religious indoctrination or even our emotions: they bubble up from our subconscious, filtering into the cognitive light through experience and social support/resistance, but originating in our limbic systems - the parts of the brain that are older than reason and social facility.

This isn't opinion or theory - this is empirically-established fact. Our moral impulses, and our sociopolitical positions in turn, correlate with our deep neurological responses to threatening or distasteful sensory stimuli. The greater a person's limbic activity when presented with images of disease, decay and injury, the more likely that person is to be sociopolitically right-wing.

If that idea strikes you the wrong way, feel free to read the studies (google Jonathan Haidt, Read Montague); and if you don't trust dem liberal scientists, study it yourself: take a simple political questionnaire and a stack of pictures to the mall, stand in a corner, and have random shoppers fill out the questionnaire to establish their political position, then rank the pictures on a "disgusting" scale of 1 to 10. You'll find that the people most sensitive to disgust will be the most right-wing (the accuracy rate of this test is between 95 and 98 percent).

I propose that Paul Ryan and company are being completely genuine: they truly do believe in a system that favors the young and strong and disfavors the old and weak; they truly do believe that the sick deserve their fate, and that the wealthy deserve the finest care. Among the right-wing Evangelicals in Congress, it has been suggested that this appalling healthcare perspective is a reflection of "prosperity Gospel" - and that wouldn't surprise me at all. They truly believe that God favors his own with physical well-being, and that sickness is a sign of the Almighty's disfavor.

Where we err is in responding to this sort of thinking with contempt. If subconscious revulsion in response to the sick, weak and old is truly at the root of this moral frame - and I believe, very firmly, that it is - then Ryan and company are acting out impulses that they come by naturally. Their minds are built to work this way. In the prehistoric past, they wouldn't be stripping their clan of protection, they would be doing the opposite - using their high sensitivity to disgust to filter out bad meat and tainted water.

Should they be in power? Of course not. Are they offering the nation something that is good for all, on any level? Of course not. But are they nefarious, evil men, intent on bringing about the deaths of citizens by the tens of thousands? Of course not. Like all of us, they are acting as their ancient brains instruct them to act, in an environment for which their ancient brains are not suited at all.

What, then, should our response be?

1. Dial down our outrage.
2. Recover our empathy.
3. *Vote...*

Interchangeable Fact and Opinion

One of the hallmarks of our contemporary dilemma is the denial of fact. So frequently do we hear fact denied by some authoritative talking head that we could stand just about anywhere, throw a baseball and hit one.

The sidestep to avoid outright denial is for the denier to demote the fact to "opinion," thereby neatly navigating around outright conflict while leaving the door open for later revision without contradiction. This technique is both clean and insidious, keeping matters of fact out of the arena of confrontation while eroding the confidence of the onlooker in what should be counted upon.

More insidious still is the reciprocal act, the elevation of opinion to fact, an act that doesn't simply diminish the effectiveness of critical thought - it removes it altogether.

Though this interchangeability of fact and opinion has been with us for millennia (the Catholic Church has, of course, been the pacesetter, but is by no means the only institutional practitioner), we have now reached a point - in the post-Enlightenment age of science! - when the leader of the free world can watch fake news TV, become agitated, tweet a random claim concocted in the moment off the top of his head, and have tens of millions of followers instantly accept it as truth, sans evidence, validation of any kind, or even the suggestion of scrutiny; moreover, any challenge of the claim or call for evidence is, by default, considered an assault on truth!

To say this behavior borders on insane is hyperbole, but just barely; how is such a thing even possible?

It is possible by means of the cognitive framework we've been discussing.

In the Paleolithic, fact and opinion were easily parsed. Facts: hyenas will kill us and eat us; fire will keep us safe at night. Opinions: the herd went left, not right; these spear points will work better than those spear points. Facts had been tested, and consistency in their acceptance and use meant survival; opinions were testable, not yet fact, and doubt necessarily led to testing.

The false opinion "I don't think this hyena will kill me" would quickly lead to death; the false fact "The herd went left, not right" would likely lead to starvation.

Once we became 'civilized' and our populations surged, the conflation of fact and opinion became possible; a powerful ruler could declare a fact to be opinion, or an opinion fact, and have the effects of an error phased away through obfuscation and sycophancy. This jumped out in stark relief when humankind crafted a means of establishing fact objectively - Science - and all groups and leaders threatened by its findings went into high gear, self-preserving their carefully-crafted illusions through fact-opinion interchange.

Here's what's going on: we've talked about cognitive clusters, the huddling of people of a particular cognitive type into social groups, for the safety and comfort of mutual reflections. Within such groups, cognitive dissent disrupts the stability of the group; even the slightest disagreement can result in the group splitting in two (it is for this reason that extremist political groups and religions stress 'purity' and 'loyalty' above all other moral values).

Opinion is promoted to fact when the opinion is that of the group's leader or when it enables, empowers or exalts the group; as a fact, it becomes social glue, strengthening group solidarity. When a fact threatens group solidarity, weakening its social glue, it is demoted to opinion, to dampen the threat.

Once an opinion is made fact or a fact is made opinion, no corrective mechanism is possible; such a mechanism compromises confidence in the group's leadership, diminishes 'purity' and weakens its social bonds. Denial not only must be maintained but intensified, lest the group perish. Any attempt at correction is considered a threat.

This all sounds pretty demoralizing, and it is, when we consider just how much cognitive clustering occurs in our social universe. But above we see the worst-case scenario: some groups are novelty-seeking, and open to change; others do not include threat-scanning, and are less inclined to fear new information.

Finally, we can take a new view of science itself, which is agnostic to cognitive types: a fact established by science is necessarily a fact, regardless of what one particular group or cognitive type thinks of it. We can even say that science is our surest hedge against the fact-opinion interchange effect - though, by definition, several of the cognitive types would naturally feel threatened by that assertion.

Understanding all of this, however, is just the first step in responding, and rectifying this terrible imbalance in reality: for the hyenas of our world are deadlier than ever, and the forks in our path forward have multiplied...

We Are Fragile

Our discussion of how each of us has differences in our brains that make our thoughts and feelings about self and others different has occurred within the context of humanity misplaced. For the past 500 generations, our kind has lived within a social universe for which our social brains are not at all suited.

This means that we are experiencing lives that are far less than they might have been, for the societies we created, as the world warmed and daily bread became a given, are not universally equitable. Our social brains were not build for inequality, bigotry, misogyny, sexual repression and threadbare intimacy. Our social brains, for many thousands of generations, facilitated strong cooperation and altruism, deep communication and intimacy, gender equality and universal kinship. It is in this social environment that human beings thrive, and would naturally be happiest.

We strive, subconsciously, to recreate that world every day. All of our clans-by-choice - church groups, fan communities - labor to revive that sense of kinship and intimacy, that comforting mutual support; civic alliances cultivate our sense of cooperation, providing an invigorating thrill of mutual achievement. Liberal altruism offers the deep satisfaction in giving of our own resources to those who have less, even when they are total strangers.

This is who we are, struggling to be, yet tightly bound and constrained in a society that lessens us.

In Haiti, there are small children begging in the streets who are crippled for life - their limbs broken by their own parents at birth, to make them more effective street beggars. The cold societies we've constructed do the same to us all - breaking us before we even begin to grow, and forcing our growth along terrible paths that drain us of empathy and reign in our compassion and cooperation, limiting our shared potential to the barest dribble of real humanity. We hobble in the streets, begging one another for a bare minimum of emotional coin, a pittance of connection - crippled for life.

Why is he saying these things?

I'm saying these things to frame a suggestion: the next time we are annoyed, vexed, infuriated over something some idiot posts online (surely sometime this afternoon)... the next time we scowl at someone we see in the mall, treating their companion callously... the next time someone at work does something nefarious or manipulative... the next time we feel disapproval and self-righteousness swelling in our bosom...

Remember: that person is crippled - as crippled as I am...

Clinical Name-Calling

Calling someone a narcissist or a sociopath is not the same as calling them a doodyhead. The latter is a very generalized epithet that can mean anything you want it to mean; the former are clinical terms with very specific diagnostic criteria, the province of behavioral science professionals.

Why does this matter? Because we're slinging these terms around very freely these days, describing particular Authoritarians rising to power around us. We can't scroll through our news feeds without seeing the word 'narcissist' these days, usually applied to the current president (or a member of his party, at the very least).

And while this is both very understandable and, more often than not, accurate, it is unadvisable, all the same; while even the nation's behavioral science professionals are breaking their own rule (the Goldwater Rule) and speaking out publicly about the implications of the president's overt, uncensored behaviors, 'narcissism' and 'sociopathy' are still highly specific pathologies orbiting highly specific personality features that are not to be taken lightly, or diagnosed randomly by drive-by counselors. Doodyhead, by contrast, is not even to be found in the Diagnostic and Statistical Manual of Mental Disorders. At least not the last time I looked.

The problem is this: if we, the voting public, start playing so fast and loose with such powerful, serious words, then we start over-applying them - first to politicians, then to public persons of all kinds, and then to each other. It's even fair to say that this has already been the case for a while, and I argue that it makes us worse, not better: when we decide, arbitrarily or second-hand, that someone out there is lacking in empathy, we tend to turn off our own empathy, as well. And we are living in times that call for more empathy from each of us, not less.

So the next time you see someone on television, or in your newsfeed, or on the sidewalk in front of you, for that matter, don't give in to the diagnostic impulse...

...stick with doodyhead.

Body Language Deficits

Whether one lives on the Left or the Right, in between, or somewhere off the map, we can all agree - surely? - that dialog on the Internet deprives us of the richness of in-person communication... body language, vocal tone, and all the other intimate cues that pass along messages from others and stir our responses.

We all get hot and bothered at times, when we see a post that just spits in the face of all we know to be true, and espouses all that we despise. We all have been in the position of firing off a hot reply, every bit as inflammatory as what triggered us - and often have hit 'Post' without stopping to think twice.

Worse, we've all had the experience of posting something we *thought*was benign and inoffensive, trigger-free, only to have one or more people go berserk over whatever it was we posted, to our utter bafflement.

And we all have defended self or others, at one point, walking something back by saying, "It didn't come across the way I intended; if you'd seen my face and heard my voice, you'd have known I didn't mean to start anything."

And that defense is very, very valid, very important. It underscores that human beings evolved to communicate in person, reading each other's eyes, faces and tone of voice, long before words were even invented:

"By signaling through fine-tuned muscles of the face and other body language, emotional approval and disapproval could be rapidly and very sensitively conveyed," writes epidemiologist Donna Armstrong of the human past. "Our first language - even of contemporary humans - is reading and responding to the unspoken emotional cues and signals of other people. We constantly practice an ancient, highly nuanced body language with each other."

Some studies have estimated that 93% of our meaning is lost when our eyes, faces and voices are removed from our communication with others. That's a fuzzy number, but whatever the reality, we certainly lose a lot when we aren't speaking face-to-face.

What can be done?

A single rule of thumb can greatly improve our digital dialogs, even if nothing can truly fix the problem altogether (short of communicating via video at all times): in every online communication, ask yourself, "Am I reacting, or am I responding?"

Reaction is purely emotional, bubbling up from the limbic system. It is immediately, unreflective, thoughtless. More often than not, when we are simply reacting, we don't say what we really mean - we don't convey what we truly wish to get across in our reply.

Response is different. Response comes from the cortex, our center of emotional stability and deliberative thought. When a reply issues from this place, it is basically an emotional reaction that has been reviewed and carefully considered - it stops being just a reaction.

Emojis help; though crude and often vague, they can sometimes offset an unfortunate phrasing and stop the person on the receiving end from jumping to a wrong conclusion. But they're a far cry from an in-person twinkle of the eye or an actual tear.

We can't change the nature of the Internet - it is a marketplace of digital dialog, for better or worse, a transmitter of ideas without human aura, and must remain so, for the foreseeable future. What we can do, however, is pledge to ourselves to move away from mere reaction, and into the more human realm of response...

Attention Magnets

There are a number of natural cognitive impulses that exist in everyone, to greater or lesser degrees. We've argued that these impulses are often unproductively repurposed, both accidentally and by design, by our social groups and by larger forces in society.

We can't exactly change our own predispositions, and we certainly can't change those of others. What good, then, is an understanding of cognitive predisposition?

Consider that *all* cognitive types are built out of human cognitive traits that serve the same function: they are Attention Magnets.

Attention is the dial that directs our thought, emotion, our reasoning, our cognitive effort. The impulses that define our cognitive predispositions all serve the function of redirecting our attention.

A Threat-Scanner's attention serves to focus the scanner on danger; a Novelty-Seeker's attention serves to redirect to the new and different; an Authoritarian's attention focuses on the words and actions of the social leader, and so on.

That's something I can work with. If I'm in a staff meeting, trying to work with others to solve a problem, and Bob has stalled the discussion with objections, I can remember that Bob is a Threat-Scanner; it is his inclination to seek out risk and danger and looming failure. Working with this, I can focus on his objections, lowering the level of threat to a point where he is less inwardly drawn and more open.

If the threat is something more abstract, such as a new policy that would diminish his department's budget, he will find straw-man reasons to object, and we will likewise get nowhere. What can I do? I can work with the new policy on the table, thinking of ways to disseminate the cost of its implementation.

Bob's type-driven responses have helped the discussion, in the end, and my direct response to them has helped as well. I've diminished the pull of the magnet that has his attention, to a useful degree.

If Janice is in the meeting and spinning up alternatives as fast as she can think of them, then I'm reminded that Janice is a Novelty-Seeker - she will bounce from shiny thing to shiny thing, given a chance. My response is simple: I speak up and draw the group's attention to the most promising of her novelties, which not only redirects her attention, but kicks her into 'hyper focus' - a trait often seen in Novelty-Seekers. Now her novelty impulse will focus her attention on the details of how her idea might work, rather than dragging her off to the next idea.

Now we're getting somewhere. We can't change other people, and we can only change ourselves with great difficulty. What we *can* do is boost cooperation, while lessening the detrimental effects of type-driven thinking, by recognizing them in others and working with them, rather than against them, to achieve the best group outcomes...

Withering Winds

Modern human minds tend not to notice improvement in self and others; and they tend to exaggerate signs of decline in self and others.

This finding, by O'Brien and Klein at the University of Chicago, carries staggering implications. Applied to ourselves, it explains why so often we shoot ourselves in the foot, whether we're trying to lose weight, attract a new partner or get a promotion; applied to others, it explains why so many people struggle to change and fail, when family and peers are cynical about their attempts.

Applied to our social and politics biases - *wow*. Just sit and think about it for 30 seconds.

How often do we observe our leaders reaching for a big change and only managing one or two steps forward, and judge them to be weak and ineffective? How many times do we observe them miss the mark, or make a public mistake, and judge them to be worthless? How many times do we look at members of another political party and amplify their less-desirable features by a factor of 100, while judging any conciliatory act to be disingenuous or even accidental?

O'Brien and Klein are calling us out - our tendency to dismiss positives and embrace negatives defeats us on every level. We know this within ourselves: it's a struggle to lose even a few pounds; getting the notice of an attractive person or one's workplace superior often requires herculean effort. How tough is it to realize that this is true for us all?

It's also helpful to note that change, whether within ourselves, others, or political parties, requires more than just will; it requires new skills, shifted awareness, and often cooperation, persistence, and monumental energy. And we often undertake it under the withering winds of skepticism issuing from friends and family.

We do ourselves a favor when we give ourselves credit for even the smallest step; and we do others an even bigger favor when we stop contributing to the wind.

Believing as My Tribe Believes

I was raised ultra-conservative, literally surrounded by ultra-conservatives into my early teens, and was exposed perpetually to the tribal beliefs of conservatives - and, at the same time, the tribal beliefs of fundamentalists. And at the same time, I was exposed to many beliefs that my birth tribe held about those outside the tribe.

High school made me doubt what I had been told about outsiders, and college clinched it: not only were my tribe's beliefs about other tribes and outsiders not true, my tribe's beliefs didn't even match the objective definitions accepted by the world at large.

This is true of most social tribes, not just conservatives: when people cluster into social groups that reflect their own thinking, they necessarily amputate the group's social objectivity. It becomes impossible to see others for who they really are: there are gaps, sometimes huge ones, in the group's perception, because of the contrived uniformity of social thought. So the tribe just fills in those gaps, very conveniently, very self-aggrandizingly. So it must be, in cognitive clusters.

On the other hand, few social groups are absolute clusters; while any cognitive cluster will be primarily composed of some central cognitive type, there will always be some similar secondary types in the mix - and these minds will vary somewhat from the core thought. And across the board, in any social group, like minds are not identical minds (there is no such thing as two identical minds): even like minds can differ considerably.

When members of a social group outsource their belief to the group or group leader, then, they are not always truly conforming: there will always be some who are just giving lip service to group belief, for the sake of group membership; some who doubt, but fear expressing their doubts to other group members; some who don't fully understand the group belief; and some who go along simply because they have no personal experience that challenges the group belief.

Group belief, in such an environment, isn't belief at all. "Belief," as a function of cognition, is experiential in nature; it is an evolutionary survival tool that sets up expectation of future events, to inform our reactions. When belief is outsourced, it stops being useful.

And belief outsourced to a uniform point of view is more dangerous still: by definition, it *cannot* represent reality; it can, at best, only convey shadows and tidbits of reality.

Beliefs are not things we actively choose, in the end; they are explanations of how our minds respond. But those responses are filtered through our social choices, and we do have some degree of control over those.

If we want our beliefs about others to represent reality, then, our best bet is to set aside those beliefs handed to us by others; we get closer to seeing people as they really are when we allow our beliefs about them to emerge from our experience of knowing them...

"You can't connect the dots looking forward; you can only connect them looking backwards. So you have to trust that the dots will somehow connect in your future. You have to trust in something – your gut, destiny, life, karma, whatever."

~Steve Jobs

Planned Detachment

Our society, mobile and misaligned as it is, doesn't just diminish intimacy between us; it actively plans for and prepares us for disconnection.

It is assumed our families will be impermanent; it is assumed that relationships are transitory. It is convenient for us to grow apart. We have even contrived a social universe where economic forces make it almost essential to do so.

This is not how human beings live best. Not only are we the most social creatures on earth, but we are creatures who developed as we did by growing together, not apart; by cultivating, from earliest childhood, bonds and intimacies with others that withstood the very worst the world could throw at us.

If we're lucky, we all have one or two such relationships - an extremely strong marriage (very rare, especially now), a childhood friendship that grew stronger through the years. But these are the exceptions, far from the rule, which is that relationships are, if not disposable, certainly very replaceable.

Society actively weans us from deep connection, almost from birth: infants are routinely separated from their parents, conveniently stored in nurseries; growing children are sequestered almost exclusively with each other (gak!). In the distant past, rites of passage were about deepening connection, not preparation for separation. Today, broken connection and emotional distance have been utterly normalized.

But in the Paleolithic era, there were no nurseries; no grade schools; no commencements, no job transfers – there was only the group, from birth to death. No planned separation, no ending of relationships. We were in it for each other, for life, deeply connected.

It's easy to argue that since we've never lived that way, we just don't know what we're missing. But a moment's thought clues us in: so prevalent is the pain we still suffer at separation and broken connection, despite its ubiquity, that we have yet to contrive a universal remedy. It is, in our age of multiple careers and rampant divorce, an epidemic.

We just aren't built to live this way. Our social minds are constructed for deep connection, for long-term camaraderie, for mutual devotion. We each have at least a little of that - but our legacy is to have much more.

There is good news, however; though we live in a world filled with too many doors and endless paths leading us away - it is still entirely up to us whether to take them or leave them...

Competing Moralities

From the *Huffington Post*, regarding Paul Ryan's Affordable Care Act replacement:

"What Ryan is 'repealing' and 'replacing' isn't a health care bill — he's swapping out the moral universe that gave birth to the Affordable Care Act with the one that he prefers. One in which the state rewards affluence and punishes those who fail to achieve it."

Ryan, the ACA and healthcare issues aside, the article is touching on an essential point that is almost always missed in the tussle of political rhetoric and socioeconomic debate. It is easy, not to mention tempting, to denounce those in our society who labor so ceaselessly in the service of preserving and increasing inequality - those who strip away protection of the poor and weak, bolstering the wealth and security of the already-wealthy and secure, all the while shaking their heads over the dubious values of the unfortunate, and congratulating themselves for teaching them an important lesson about bootstraps. We want to knock such people off their high horse, to slap them silly, to hold a mirror up to them and give them a glimpse of true moral deficit.

The problem isn't specific to inequality; it permeates our sociopolitical discourse, from racism to misogyny to the role of government. It truly is a problem with the concept of morality, and it can't be solved in the context of any one of these issues.

Ryan and his GOP cohorts are viewed by their opponents as shills for the rich, loathing of their own constituents, oppressors of the downtrodden. From their point of view, the political right manages to blame every ill of society on its weakest members. And this seems dreadfully immoral, from the outside looking in. The anger is understandable, but the point is missed if those critics fail to fully grasp that their opponents are, indeed, acting from their own moral framework.

We could get into the weeds of right-wing moral assumptions, but the broader point is more important: people living in cognitive clusters don't just share their own versions of fact and opinion; they share a common perception of human nature.

And our perception of human nature, of the inner workings of human behaviors, choices and the values that drive them, forms the framework of our shared morality. Within our in-groups, we parse right and wrong by way of how we classify the behaviors of others - what we observe. It has little to do with what actually drives behavior, which we seldom can see.

Deeper still, we assume a great deal about the inner workings of others based on our own hidden voices. Jonathan Haidt and others have done considerable research in this area, uncovering the uncomfortable fact that our moral leanings derive from our deepest subconscious emotions - limbic impulses that define what attracts us and repels us. What attracts us is, deep in our minds, good; what repels us is evil; and we assign 'good' and 'evil' to others, based on whether their own impulses agree or disagree with our own. How do we know we're right? The people who agree with us tell us so.

Understanding this is no solution, of course; it gets us no closer to persuading Paul Ryan that his disdain for those at the bottom is turpitude on a bed of lettuce. If anything, it makes matters worse, because we realize that those against whom we struggle are not simply foot soldiers in the armies of avarice; they are warriors willing to march into hell for their heavenly cause. No argument, no debate, no headline, no rhetoric, no amount of outrage, no bipartisan bargain will ever dislodge them; nor will any spin from their side ever change the fact that such moral beachheads have nothing to do, ultimately, with public policy.

We can only solve the problem of disparate moralities by turning humankind away from the practice of cognitive clustering - the work of decades, if it's achievable at all. But at a more local level, we can push back against competing moralities by the simple act of learning from them.

In the case of Ryan and the threat to healthcare: go into the voting booth, repeal, replace...

(Turn to Page 193)

Mom and Dad Are Splitting Up[6]

Here we stand, worlds apart, hearts broken in two ...

The Journey reference will not be lost on my friends, and anyone else who reads me will not be terribly surprised by what follows.

The United States has become like a house where Mom and Dad are at war, ready to destroy each other, with one or the other poised to abandon all the kids. And while some are indulging that red-hot rancor Mom and Dad are feeling toward each other, most of us feel like the kids who are being ripped to pieces by the feud, trapped in the middle day in and day out.

Dad likes to cast this tragic battle in terms of Good and Evil. Mom casts it in terms of Informed and Ignorant. Both have surrendered dialog for rhetoric. And both wear golden handcuffs.

It would be encouraging if this terrible domestic quarrel boiled down to Good vs. Evil – but we don't really have definitions of those words that everyone can agree on anymore, if we ever did. Certainly Dad seems as stupid as is humanly possible, if he thinks his declaration of himself as Good and Mom as Evil will impress anybody other than his drinking buddies. Informed/Ignorant is demonstrably valid, but by its very nature is insurmountable within the household. How can Mom possibly expect her pronouncement of Dad's ignorance to hold sway with anyone who actually *is* ignorant (including, and especially, Dad)?

And it's a deep relief to think that loosening the golden handcuffs which bind them together might open the doors and windows of this dysfunctional home, and bring the sunlight and fresh air of reason, sanity and harmony.

But that turns out not to be the case.

Politics! The art and science of government, overseeing the safety and prosperity of a nation/state, defending its citizens and their rights;

---

[6] Originally published in the blog "That Turns Out Not to Be the Case," May 27, 2012

optimizing resources, protecting the populace, improving the quality of life for all. That's the theory, anyway.

Mom and Dad are at war, not over their ultimate objectives, but over their priorities, it seems. Don't they both want the kids to be safe? Healthy? Adequately cared for? Don't they both cherish their children's future, and want better for the kids and their generation than they themselves have enjoyed? Isn't their battle, at the heart of it, about how to get there, rather than where they're going?

If that's true, then Good v. Evil is bullshit, and needs to be called out. If it's about priorities, rather than objectives, then Dad gets a slap on the wrist – no, across the chops – for dishonoring Mom. Shame on him! Surely it is not "evil" to want the best for the kids, but to differ on how to achieve it. And while she can call Dad "ignorant" (and a number of other colorful adjectives) for believing such a dumb thing, Mom is lost in the tall grass – and not as "informed" as she might want to think she is – if she thinks that calling Dad "ignorant" is going to advance her priorities, however right she might be.

Politics is, ideally, about advancing human well-being, and if we dispense with Mom and Dad's rhetoric of Good/Evil, Informed/Ignorant, we are left with the less-threatening problem of Difference in Approach — but Mom and Dad are seeking the same thing, right?

Self-Interest. For each of us, our partners, our kids.

From Adam Smith to Thomas Hobbes to Bishop Joseph Butler, "Self-Interest" is the driver. The general idea is that if each person pursues what works for them, we wind up with a society where the betterment of all is achieved. This conceptual rule rests at the core of our politics, our economics, our sense of how the world should work. We hold that truth to be self-evident, that politics and economics rely upon the assumption that Nations, Communities and People *all* act in accordance with their own self-interest.

But… that turns out not to be the case.

When we take a step closer, we find that it isn't much about Self-Interest at all. According to George Lakoff (et al), we don't really decide on the basis of

Self-Interest, but on the basis of Identity. Often, Self-Interest and Identity overlap, which obscures the truth of our general motivations. We have years of analysis of voter behavior and self-report at this point which deliver a new picture: if faced with voting their socioeconomic self-interest or voting their identity, when the two do not coincide, most people will tend to vote identity. And this is no surprise to the career politician, who has been using this truth to manipulate voters for centuries.

Lakoff offers a compelling example. In the 2003 California gubernatorial recall election, Gray Davis was pitted against actor Arnold Schwarzenegger, who took the governor's office from him without running on the issues, and despite massive amounts of effort on the part of labor to educate the voting public on Davis's policies. Those policies were far more in the interests of the working voter than Schwarzenegger's, but Davis is a poor communicator, an often-fatal flaw for a politician.

We all know how it turned out, but what's interesting to Lakoff is data gathered from the focus groups at the exit polls. Union workers were presented with the two opposing labor policies, and asked, "Which of these works better for you?" Consistently, they responded, "The Davis one."

Then they were asked who they were voting for. "Arnold!!!"

If our political and economic behavior is, at its core, more about Who We Are than What We Need, then the battle between Mom and Dad begins to make a lot more sense. Who We Are isn't about issues or resources or policies; it's about the features of our personalities, and our mis/understanding of them in other people.

Political warfare, when you strip away the rhetoric and the propaganda and the talk-radio blowhards, is personality warfare.

This seems like cause for real hope, doesn't it? If this thing with Mom and Dad isn't really about "Good" and "Evil," and if it isn't priorities, or even the issues that they're bickering over – if it's about Who They Are, their personalities, then things can change! Mom and Dad can decide to be different, and everything will be better.

Well … that turns out not to be the case.

What are the core features of your personality? Are you an introvert or an extrovert? Are you comfortable with routine, or do you like to shake things up? Do you love being part of a crowd, or are you more solitary? Did you choose these things, or are they just traits you were born with?

Some of those personality features form the core of our social/political selves. For instance, a person can be risk-averse, or a risk-taker; change-averse, or a novelty-seeker; approval-seeker or indifferent to reward. All of these personality traits map to social and political behavior.

If you're a cautious person, did you choose that trait, or did it choose you? If you're a novelty-seeker, compelled to scan the horizon for the new and different, did you wake up one morning and decide to be that way, or has it always been a part of you? We don't attain the age of reason and go to the mall and try on personalities; we are born with a set of natural propensities, and our early lives shape them, and in our adult lives, they define our social selves. Certainly we can make choices about which aspects of our personalities we choose to develop or not, but the raw material has to be there in the first place. And that's not something we can just pick.

If it's down to things we're born with, we're in luck: we've had a ring-side seat at the mapping of the human genome, and it's told us a great deal about how all this works. For instance, we know that novelty-seeking – the basis of creativity – is a consequence of lower levels of dopamine in the brain, which means that people who have this lower dopamine level will naturally seek more stimulation from the world around them in order to feel "right" – where people with higher levels will not seek that stimulation, and will naturally prefer a more orderly, less-stimulating environment. And we have genes for that: DRD4 and its cousins.

Dopamine is just one of many flavors of brain food that define how we emerge in the world, alongside serotonin, norepinephrine and others. And enough research has already been done to assure us that the recipes our brains concoct do indeed form the first chapter of the story of Who We Are. But it isn't that simple (not that behavioral genetics is anywhere close to "simple"). Isn't Nurture the flip side of Nature? It absolutely is, as when we factor a high-dopamine child raised by two high-dopamine parents, and have that need-for-order ratcheted up in the child's emerging social self – or the opposite, a low-dopamine child born to high-dopamine parents, a story more likely to end in dashed expectations and misunderstanding, which add new features to the personalities of all. It isn't simple, but at least we're in the right room.

So Mom and Dad are splitting up. And in the end, it's about Who They Are and things they can't change, and wouldn't want to change, and *shouldn't* change, within themselves and each other. It's about a lack of understanding, an inability to see, a tragic loss of connection that shapes how they see the world, themselves, and each other (and all the rest of us). They would have one path left back to each other, if the knowledge of what's really going on between them could cross their growing rift. The power of knowledge has lit up the world for us, and with understanding can come a softening of our hardened feelings toward each other, a calmer and more mutually compassionate channeling of our emotional energies as we continually build the world. If only that knowledge could penetrate those deep genetic barriers to true shared understanding that all of us harbor.

But that turns out not to be the case …

Warm Hands

Looking around, observing the ratcheting-up of tensions and anger, can be discouraging. Our emotions, biases, attitudes and beliefs come from a place deep within, beyond the reach of rhetoric and indoctrination - and this should ratchet up our compassion for all, rather than increase our anger burn.

All around me, people are angry. My closest friends are angry, my colleagues are angry. My family is angry. As diligently as I can, I've been writing and speaking and trying to turn that tide, trying to emphasize that our anger is misplaced, our understanding of what we are experiencing is incomplete. Now is not the time for anger or fear or outrage - now is the time for pursuit of deeper knowledge and perception of *why* the things we are seeing are occurring, so that we can meaningfully address them with true long-term solutions, rather than desperate, in-the-moment deflections.

There's another reason: the angrier and more afraid we get, the less rational we become. That is not a phenomenon of red or blue brains, that is a trait shared by *all* brains - anger and fear constrict our attention to the options Fight and Flight, and neither will save us in this case. We need to turn off fear and anger and turn on reason and insight.

But I can find very few willing to even hear that argument, let alone embrace it; outrage keeps one warm, fear can be a kind of thrill, and anger is an Identity marker. People prefer their outrage, regardless of their political stripe; it makes them feel good.

But this is not the moment for such indulgences. This is the moment for deep breaths and adult resolve. The house is burning; we can warm our hands in other ways.

Sin, Virtue and Cro-Magnon Supremacy

It is commonly assumed – and, unfortunately, frequently taught in classrooms – that Cro-Magnon humans (prehistoric people like us) prevailed over the Neandertals and other early humans by way of aggressive dominance or superior brainpower.

This turns out not to be the case. While a number of factors led to Cro-Magnon supremacy in the ancient world (see Best Friends, elsewhere in this book), brainpower was close to a wash (Neandertal brains were slightly larger, ours were slightly more creative); and we now know that the notion of our "Killer Ape" legacy was far off base.

What was it, apart from our affinity for pets, that made us more survival-worthy?

The common conception is that modern humans are simply more aggressive and determined. The real answer: it was our altruism and cooperation.

The old school of anthropology (which includes some modern thinkers even now, like Steven Pinker) see humanity's rise as a steady climb out of barbarism into enlightened cooperation – a very self-congratulatory assumption, and easy to derive from a superficial survey of the archeological record. But those answers are too easy: social creatures – more specifically, eusocial creatures (see Eusocial, elsewhere in this book) – are more complex, and therein lies part of our answer.

Biologist Edward O. Wilson has described the evolutionary march of eusocial creatures as selective on both individual and group levels; that is, individual actions and responses affect selection, but so do adaptive behaviors driven by group dynamics.

And one of those adaptive behaviors is altruism – selfless concern for the well-being of other group members.

Contemporary game theory provides great insight into the strategic effects of selfish behavior over altruistic behavior. When it's person against person, the advantages of selfishness over cooperation often prevail. This can be demonstrated mathematically as well as in experimental scenarios with people.

At the group level, per Wilson, it swings the other way:

"[In early human evolution] a conflict ensued between individual-level selection, with individuals competing with other individuals in the same group, on the one side, and group-level selection, with competition among groups, on the other. The latter force promoted altruism and cooperation among all the group members. It led to innate group-wide morality and a sense of conscience and honor. The competition between the two forces can be succinctly expressed as follows: Within groups selfish individuals beat altruistic individuals, but groups of altruists beat groups of selfish individuals. Or, risking oversimplification, individual selection promoted sin, while group selection promoted virtue."[7]

All the proto-human species of genus Homo were exceptionally cooperative; as brain size increased, however, from the tiny minds of Homo habilis to the intermediate skulls of Homo erectus to our own really big brains, awareness and knowledge of our kin greatly increased, and with them, our level of cooperation and altruistic behavior. By the time of the European showdown between Neandertal and Cro-Magnon, altruistic cooperation was our defining factor – as evidenced by our emerging ability to extend it to our four-legged companions.

Every step up the evolutionary ladder, from bipedalism on, has seen an increase in our levels of altruistic cooperation. Our ability to empathize with our kin and sacrifice for their well-being essentially extends the love of parent for child throughout the tribe, resulting in astonishingly strong bonds – bonds that have seen us through endless chaos and danger, whirlwinds of climate change, and a steady march across a perpetually shifting landscape.

---

[7] In his book *The Meaning of Human Existence*, Liveright, 2015

Homo sapiens won out, achieving the pinnacle (so far) in altruistic feelings for one another. Those feelings, and the behaviors that came with them, got us to where we are today. How ironic that we seem to be abandoning them.

Human Nature, Once Again

If I am doing a complex calculation, and my initial value is off, the entire calculation will be off.

If I am in a laboratory, synthesizing a new molecule, and I use the wrong base molecule, I will not end up with the molecule I am trying to create.

Similarly, if I am creating or maintaining institutions and policies that affect human lives, and my perception of human nature is not accurate, the institutions and policies can never be universally effective, and will at best serve some subset of people, rather than all.

It follows that those who lead, those who create policy and those who implement services and social infrastructure have not just an advantage but a serious obligation in the area of human nature. To seek out the most accurate perception and base policy, service and action on that perception becomes a primary responsibility, precedent to everything else, and a serendipitous path to greater success.

It further follows that those of us who select our leaders, by voting for them or supporting them, etc., select best when we ourselves seek that more accurate take on human nature, and choose leaders who move in that direction.

How do we accomplish this?

First, we realize that our own inner picture of humankind is necessarily too limited to be accurate, let alone all-inclusive; the best we can normally do is to passively believe that how we view the world - and other people - is how it really is, when it really isn't - and let that view go, inwardly committing to seek out a better one.

Next, we reject the portrait of human nature presented by any one group, be it religious, political, ideological or otherwise. Most of these groups have at their very heart an emotional attachment to their version of what a human being is, and each of those versions is as limited as any individual's perception, no matter how systematically presented - because social groups echo each other's thinking, often (even especially) when that thinking is incorrect.

Finally, we have to recognize that any perception of human nature that's rooted in reality is necessarily going to reflect the diversity that underlies all those different viewpoints. It's precisely because human beings see things differently that human nature cannot be accurately captured in a lone snapshot - whatever we define human nature to be, diversity is unquestionably a primary ingredient.

That we are all different, and that the differences are never necessarily 'right' or 'wrong' must take its place at the center of our regard for and service to one another. Along that path lies a better understanding of self and others, of how best to deploy our collective efforts, and the surest hand in meeting one another's needs.

Hereditary Belief

There is a sociologist named Tony Campolo who is also a pastor in the US evangelical community. For decades he has been a force for liberal Christianity, advocating for social justice as a speaker and writer. His son Bart followed in his footsteps, also becoming a pastor, also advocating for social justice.

There came a day when Bart Campolo looked in the mirror and realized that while he found the Christian ethic admirable, he really didn't honestly believe the Bronze Age myths that accompanied it. While many career pastors who experience such awakenings keep them to themselves, Campolo was very transparent and forthcoming. The resulting stir in the evangelical community led to a book co-authored with his father – *Why I Left, Why I Stayed.*

An unapologetic and compassionate exercise, the book is most notable for its exceptionality: It is an oasis of calm and mutual respect in the fundamentalist wasteland of exaggerated piety, moral posturing and tribal chest-thumping. It is an intimate portrait of a father and son who love each other and very much want to bridge the gulf between them, a gulf that is completely imaginary from one point of view, and of ultimate significance from the other.

The Campolo boys will be just fine, in the end, but their experience illuminates an interesting human social feature: hereditary belief.

Without exception, the patriarchal monotheistic religions require devout parents to raise up their children in their own faith; it is a given, even without the supporting text. From the standpoint of the institution, this is of course wise; the Catholic Church wants all Catholic couples to generate many new young Catholics, etc. It's a long-term survival strategy for the group.

But what is happening in the relationships themselves? What exactly is 'belief?' Why is it so important, in this context? Is transmission of belief through family inheritance a valid feature of intimate relationships?

Tony Campolo is typical of parents in the evangelical community: he and his wife raised their son to believe as they do, without even questioning whether it was the right thing or best thing for him. Alternately, many parents beyond the evangelical community let their children make up their own minds about religion, being honest about their own convictions but permitting the child to explore different ways of thinking as they will. Which is best, if either?

There is no absolute answer, but it is informative to dig down to 'belief' itself.

At its most basic, a 'belief' is the social framing of an expectation – a pre-factual, pre-experiential assumption about the world or other people. Beliefs are often supported by experience and fact, but can exist independent of both. And it is a strength of human social evolution that belief can be transmitted through a group in lieu of experience: "I believe the lion will eat me if it catches me in the open," for instance, is absolutely something we would rather acquire from others, rather than through personal experience.

Projecting belief into the future, into relationships, and ultimately into our own behavioral choices leverages expectation as the paintbrush we use to paint our models of reality, each in our own minds. Having beliefs tested against experience, especially when alternative beliefs are in competition, strengthens our understanding of the world and each other, to the benefit of all.

In the case of the Campolo family, we really can't get anywhere with this: Tony's belief in the unobservable and the untestable can never have a measurable consequence in their relationship. His worst parental fear – that Bart will go to hell – is ultimately just that, a fear, with an unknowable outcome. The one thing we can be certain of is this: the chasm between them is of no consequence at all to the world around them. Both men will continue to serve humankind, each in his own way and to the best of his ability, to his dying day.

The broader consequences of hereditary belief, however, are not so easily wrapped up. Looking at the practical functionality of belief in ancient terms, its strength is its usefulness in testing reality. That testing, that constant ratcheting of belief toward observable facts about the real world and other people, strengthens us and better equips us to survive and thrive.

When belief is inherited, handed down from parent to child with no testing, no challenge, no review of competing ideas, the belief itself can drift into the position of actually competing with reality: as a family legacy, emotional attachment to the belief can eventually outweigh an individual's commitment to experiencing the world as it really is.

Experience ceases to fine-tune understanding, because discovery becomes less necessary. And depriving a child of the experience of discovering for themselves eventually erodes their ability to discover for themselves at all.

And, finally, there is the group beyond the family. When members of a group outsource personal discovery and exploration to parental edict, the activity and process of exploration of ideas and the emotions they create within us is lost; members of the group are weaker for it; and the group itself loses strength.

When we each discover for ourselves, and are encouraged by our parents to do so, and when we then bring the fruits of our discovery into the dynamics of our group, the group grows stronger.

When parents can make this their legacy, and be accepting of their children regardless of where their exploration take them – when 'belief' is respected as personal discovery, unimposed and nurtured for the sake of the child, not the belief - families grow stronger, too.

(Turn to Page 119)

Club Human![8]

Most of us have *2001: A Space Odyssey* to thank for it, but wherever we may have picked it up, the Myth of the Caveman as Club-Wielding Brute is deeply entrenched in our cultural consciousness.

It's an iconic image: A wandering tribe of African australopithecines has a rumble with another tribe over a watering hole, and the pensive Moonwatcher, having noticed that the thigh bone of a dead boar makes a formidable extension of his own arm, proceeds to use that bone to club one of the opposing gang to death, thus committing the first murder. Flash-forward to 2001, and the image of an orbital nuclear warhead platform.

The image has stayed with us over the decades, augmented by a general cultural perception that it represents a real chunk of the human past: the idea that bloodthirsty violence was an evolutionary adaptation that got us where we are today, and that it informs our understanding of who we've come to be, a dozen years beyond 2001.

Beat It With a Stick

We've seen variations all over the place – in films, on television, in novels and comic books – and Arthur C. Clarke went out of his way to make it part of the human story he sketches out in *2001*. He was trying to make the story as factual as possible, and at the time, the idea of hominids as violent, murderous creatures represented the best thinking of anthropologists. Clarke got these ideas from author Robert Ardrey, whose popular books *African Genesis* and *The Territorial Imperative* had been best-sellers.

Ardrey had, in turn, taken the notion from the work of Australian anatomist Raymond Dart, who had turned his mind to an interesting problem and come up with a solution that seemed to answer a number of questions about both our ancient past and our contentious present. The problem Dart tackled was explaining a pile of bones in South Africa, in a place called Makapansgat.

---

[8] This essay appears under another title in *Catching the Enterprise: Achieving* Star Trek*'s Vision of the Human Future*, by the author

The Makapansgat dig was a cave containing a massive stockpile of humerus and femur bones – the long, thick, clunky ones within the upper arms and legs of mammals – and was faced with answering the question, why these bones and no others? Some of the bones were human, some were from gazelles, and so on. But beyond these, there were only fragments of other, smaller bones.

Dart's solution was elegant. The bones, he suggested, were weapons, and their cave stockpile was essentially an armory. The long, thick humerus and femur, regardless of source, make for a deadly extension of the human arm. Such a tool would confer an overwhelming advantage in a fight.

Building on this idea, Dart recast early humans as the brutes we see in our pop-culture myths: bloodthirsty killers and cannibals, ruling the African veldt as merciless packs of enraged hoodlums, cruising the savannah, spoiling for a fight. Ardrey spread this picture far and wide, all the way to Clarke, and what came to be known as the Killer Ape Theory – the idea that violence is a human default, a necessary step in our evolution – entered the public consciousness, where it remains today.

The problem is: well, it turns out not to be the case.

Cat Scratch Fever

Enter Charles Kimberlin Brain, known for some reason as "Bob," of the Transvaal Museum. Enthused by Dart's Killer Ape Theory and anxious to explore it, he sought out additional bone accumulations, similar to the one at Makapansgat. An expert in cave taphonomy (the study of environmental features and conditions), Brain was an ideal investigator to continue the work.

But what he found simply didn't fit Dart's story. In a project that stretched on year after year, as more and more specimens were examined, Brain found a pattern that turned the Dart profile of early humanity upside down: within the bone accumulation sites, those big bones – taken at first for clubs – were covered with scratches…from the teeth of cats.

The stockpiles were what remained of leopard kills, over time, the largest bones being the only ones too large for the cat's jaw to break open for their protein-rich marrow. Fragments of human skulls, also too large for munching, were likewise found in the stockpiles – and likewise bore the teeth marks of big cats. Moreover, no other human artifacts were present, none of the stone tools used by hominids at the time, when they should have been, if the cave sites were in fact hominid habitats; and no stockpiles like the ones at Makapansgat have ever been found at a site of human habitation.

Dart's picture of human brute as apex predator, then, collapsed, not many years after *2001* was released in 1968, and the Killer Ape Theory has been discarded by anthropologists, for the most part. It was the big cats – the leopard, the sabertooth and their kin – who ruled Africa as apex predators. Humankind, on its way to world dominance, remained prey in its prehistoric years. (As a footnote, Dart was delighted when he learned that his theory had been overturned, as any true scientist would be; and lest we view Brain's refutation as any sort of I-said-he-said, note that Brain spent 25 years at the task, examining well over a quarter of a million bones.)
Nor was *2001*'s image of the australopithecine Jets-Sharks rumble ever supported with anthropological evidence of intra-species warfare, or even battle between hominid competitors. If we have been beating each other's brains out with clubs for 3,000,000 years, then Africa should be riddled with archeological digs of battlegrounds.

And we don't find them in Europe, where Cro-Magnon and Neandertal had their showdown far more recently. Instead, our cousins seem to have slipped away quietly, without fuss, left not upon battlegrounds but whole, within their homes.

Why is he telling us this?

I'm telling you this because the Killer Ape Theory was disproven decades ago, yet we still see ourselves through that ghastly and disturbing filter. As well-meaning as Clarke and Kubrick (and countless other science-driven scenarists) may have been, we are still hauling around the self-image of the vicious savage, rather than that of the industrious survivor. Maybe we need a new movie, I don't know, but it's certainly time for a new narrative: one that cultivates the message, within our collective consciousness, that the murderous beasts among us are the exception, not the rule; and that we are, for the most part, determined and resourceful beings who lust not for blood, but for light.

"I've learned that people will forget what you said, people will forget what you did, but people will never forget how you made them feel."

~Maya Angelou

The Framers and Authoritarianism

The 2017 election in France occurred under the same dark cybershadow that the 2016 US election did, and it's prudent to point out the trend: the world's Authoritarian agencies are aggressively employing technology to control populations, to acquire and secure power. It's all very 1984, very disturbing, even terrifying.

It was surprising that it could even happen in the US, and I would argue that only this sort of shadowy manipulation can bring it about, and for this reason:

The Framers designed the United States in an atmosphere of rebellion against Authoritarianism. Our system of government was a rebuke of King George, but more broadly, a rebuke against arbitrary authority of any kind. Our constitution established an entirely new paradigm for human government, modeled to some degree on ancient Rome but baking in safeguards never before conceived.

First and foremost, in the US form of government, authority is distributed, decentralized; no agency of power can dominate any other. Our current president chafes at that, and his party has sought to circumvent it again and again - but that distribution of power is intended to ensure that neither he nor anyone can achieve Authoritarian dominance over the US government.

Second, the Framers designed the government to oscillate - to reboot frequently, in accommodation of shifts in public concerns and needs. No one administration or Congress persists; all are, by design, brief.

Finally, the Framers established legislative process that forces deliberative resolution of conflict and disagreement among lawmakers. Lawmaking was designed to be difficult and time-consuming, to prevent frivolous or ill-considered policy from ascending - the process requires painstaking review of all would-be law, to ensure input from all sides before voting actually occurs.

As Authoritarianism rises throughout the world, with Russia behind the curtain, we observe that Trump and his party are actively dismantling the very mechanisms the Framers devised to protect us from it. Once gone, they will be very, very difficult to restore.

Bubbles, Chambers, and Clusters: A Distinction

There's much mention in the media of "bubbles" - self-imposed insulations we observe among some social or political groups. Living in a "bubble" means that everyone on the inside is exposed only to information and ideas that are already in the bubble. It's a way of reinforcing ideas important to the group, by filtering out the contaminants of fact and skepticism.

Another term for the same phenomenon is "echo chamber," which is more or less interchangeable with "bubble," but carries a bit of additional meaning: within an "echo chamber," all opinions reflect one's own - a natural, comforting consequence of informational bubbling.

Then there's the "cognitive cluster," a term we've used quite a bit. A cognitive cluster will have among its features both informational filtering and opinion echoing - but it has several additional features, as well.

Bubbles are primarily about information. A bubble is a social insulation structure, created to sift away information that challenges the group's ideas or self-concept. Once that is achieved, the bubble has done its job. A cognitive cluster, however, is somewhat deeper: it isn't just about the filtering of information, it's about how the members of the cluster process that information.

A cognitive cluster is, by definition, a group of people who have the same (or very similar) cognitive processing styles - the same ratios of comfort/discomfort, trust/distrust, fear, group commitment, and so on. They not only want their information filtered to favor themselves and their group, or to hear their own views repeated - they want to be among people who receive that information and opinion in the same way that they do...to be among people who echo their reactions, as well.

This is not necessarily true of bubbles. The Trump Twitter bubble, for instance, is a prominent phenomenon in the online world, a place where hundreds of thousands of people go for information on the president. It necessarily contains people of many different cognitive types, including both the president's fans and opponents.

Nor are bubbles always about information: we've pointed out that they can be based on emotion (fear, for instance, re Joseph Stalin), and thus contain persons of all cognitive types. And this raises an additional distinction: while bubbles and echo chambers can contain people who are there by chance or even involuntarily, a cognitive cluster is necessarily a group that a person overtly decides to join: they are there because they want to be around those who think and feel as they do.

One thing that all of these social environments certainly have in common is this: they aren't healthy. Bubbles, echo chambers, and cognitive clusters all diminish both the healthy scrutiny of information and our ability to treat it with honest selectivity. They gradually degrade our ability to think well, and reinforce emotions that can be not only healthy but ultimately toxic.

The remedies, fortunately, are simple: don't participate, or if you do, don't participate exclusively; cultivate many sources of input into your thinking; and, if you can muster the will, push back against clustering from within - by offering new views and ideas...

The Economics of Cognitive Types

We've talked often of the different cognitive types to be found in any human population, and how those types have been around for hundreds of thousands of years. We've also talked about how all of that cognitive circuitry still exists in our brains today, even though our social universe has altered our existence in the world to the point of unrecognizability, with respect to our Paleolithic past.

We can look at our modern economic behaviors and see echoes of them in our ancient ancestors - and, conversely, look at how our ancestors lived, and get a new perspective on our modern economic behaviors.

Some cognitive types are natural pattern finders. I was reminded of the importance of this while watching the Neil deGrasse Tyson version of *Cosmos*, which emphasized how the study of the night skies informed Cro-Magnon migration patterns, hunting plans, and ultimately planting of crops. Not all cognitive types have this knack, however; others are more focused on preserving a safe status quo, on arriving in moments of stability and maintaining them. Such a mind is skilled at perpetuating beneficial conditions - keeping predators away, maintaining warmth, food supply, access to water, and so on.

The pattern-finder and the stability-maintainer are deeply dependent upon one another. The pattern-finder can reach into the environment and produce resources, which the stability-maintainer cannot; the stability-maintainer is dependent upon the pattern-finder for production. The pattern-finder, on the other hand, cannot indulge those skills along a dangerous landscape without the assurance that the stability-maintainer is taking care of business with the less-secure members of the tribe.

And so it went, for several million years: these two types (and half a dozen others) lived in a strong, cooperative equilibrium, each providing what others could not, fine-tuning survival amid constantly shifting conditions.

Until... the earth warmed, and human beings learned to create food in fixed locations.

Now the stability-maintainer's role shifts; his cognitive inclination - to secure resources - is deeply indulged, as food can now be stored for future consumption.

The pattern-finder has never worried about this, because the pattern-finder can go out and locate new food on demand. This is no longer necessary.

The two cognitive types, so long in healthy equilibrium, are no longer so: the stability-maintainer now has a mechanism by which his own cognitive impulses can be indulged beyond their actual usefulness to the group - his task is now accumulation.

The pattern-finder's cognitive impulses are now superfluous: within a few generations, they cease to bolster a group-critical skill set, and their abilities are quashed in the mundanity of farm chores.

Accumulation creates the potential for social stratification. It becomes possible for entire groups within groups to cease labor altogether, and to appoint themselves the tribal decision-makers.

And Authoritarianism is born.

Creativity in Government

We've long been aware that there is a fundamental connection between cognitive style and creativity - the study of the neurological underpinnings of creativity has been in progress for almost three decades.

This raises interesting thoughts and a few crucial questions. Is it any wonder, for instance, that the most creative people around us tend to exist in the same cognitive types? in the same quarter of the political spectrum? It's not a brag for that quarter or those types; it's just another confirmation that our inborn cognitive styles determine where we sit in the human landscape, and what we personally can see from that perspective.

Creativity relies upon several key brain components and features, all of which are genetically linked. Perhaps the most prominent is an individual's natural dopamine receptivity: low dopamine receptivity results in a person who craves environmental stimulation far beyond the norm, causing them to dig deeper and deeper into new experiences and indulge in thoughts, concepts and ideas on the frontiers of those experiences. That's how you get Beatles.

It's also illuminating to look at our sociopolitical landscape, with its elephant-in-the-room dysfunctions, ineffective ideologies and threadbare policy bromides, and factor in this creation-cognition dynamic. Put simply, conservatives tend not to be very creative, while liberals are all too creative.

The conservative lawmaker has little use for the new and different; s/he wants to return to ways of the past. The liberal lawmaker is too often infatuated with the new and different; let's try something unusual, even though what we have in place is doing just fine.

We get into trouble when what we have in place *isn't* working, or is perceived to not be working, and the tool brought forth is not creativity, but ideology; new ideas are nowhere to be found, and nothing emerges but old clichés. This is where we find ourselves right now on the ACA/repeal-replace debacle.

It is easily argued that the last creative GOP president was Nixon (triangular diplomacy), and the last true innovator was Eisenhower (merging defense initiatives with public works for economy- and security-enhancing landmark projects). And it's easy to see that liberal creativity in the White House has pushed for too-much-too-soon since LBJ - when was the last stoic Democrat in the Oval?

Once again - it can't be said too often - what is needed is balance. We *must* have new ideas...adapt or die! But we also must concentrate the innovation in those areas where we truly need it, and to leave effective policy in place, undiddled. The push-pull of liberal-conservative, accelerator and brake, makes for safe progress.

The Nation-as-Family

We've talked about the Strict Father/Nurturant Parent Morality model of sociopolitical behavior, based on the work of George Layoff. Within these frames, people tend to view leaders and the politics surrounding them, as well as decision-making in general, in the same way they view the way they were raised.

In the Strict Father model, the leader is given a patriarchal loyalty, viewed as an ultimate authority and obeyed unquestioningly. Social order is viewed, as within a Strict Father household, as a matter of authority, obedience, discipline and punishment: these stones pave the path to a moral society.

In the Nurturant Parent model, mother and father are equal, and so are the members of the family/society. Social order is a matter of the young learning from the old, cooperation being the primary tool of empowerment, and morality is an emergent feature of the meeting of mutual needs.

Here's the thing: for *either* of these models to take hold in the mind of a citizen-voter, the Nation-as-Family model must already be operative; the citizen-voter must subconsciously perceive the country to be just that, an extended family, subject to the same relationship dynamics s/he grew up with.

The Nation-as-Family metaphor is, of course, completely unworkable; families and nations have almost nothing in common, except that both are made up of human beings. But the impulse to adopt the metaphor, however passively, is unsurprising; for hundreds of thousands of years, the closest thing to a "nation" was a human clan, containing no more than a couple of hundred people at most - many of them literally family.

Put another way, we're stuck with Nation-as-Family - and so, consequently, with Strict Father and Nurturant Parent Morality models. For most of human history, the Strict Father has dominated - but it need not continue to be so. Just the awareness of these models alone, and the ability to see them at work in others, allows us to tune our words and actions in such a way as to trigger one frame or another in the minds of those we encounter - ironically, nothing more (or less) than a matter of discipline...

Paleomorality

Once again, I'm going to go out on a limb and admonish my own tribe. Progressives, liberals, Democrats –*stop* the ceaseless condemnation of the Right. *Stop* with the perpetual wails of "Hypocrisy!" and "Heartless!" and "Deplorables!"

Despite the hot water this is getting me into even with my friends, I'm moved to increase this drum beat for a couple of reasons: the first is that the science of human social behavior is marching on, oblivious to all we're experiencing, and it will continue to do so - and that science says the Left's moral outrage is faux. And the second reason is that I recently read a thread, started by a psychologist of my acquaintance, populated with conservative pronouncements about the Left - pronouncements that were, as usual, self-serving, demeaning, and utterly wrong-headed (I've yet to ever hear a conservative assessment of the worldview of a liberal that wasn't light-years removed from reality).

But I declined to join in on that thread. Surrounded daily by the gnashing of liberal-progressive teeth, I am standing on very precarious ground myself, and I am realizing more and more each day that my own tribe's moral authority is less than shiny.

It is not that my feelings about liberal-progressive values have changed; on the contrary, I embrace them more firmly than ever. But it is increasingly clear to me that my tribe has no more claim to ownership of "values" than the Evangelical chest-thumpers - "values," such as they are, are behavioral expressions of subconscious emotional responses, and the only truly definitive thing we can claim about emotional responses is that we all have them.

Nor do I feel that the behavior of the Right, in government or among the voters, is particularly admirable; if I'm rating the behavior itself, there is much to be ashamed of. I'm not excusing any of it, not in the slightest. Watching the Trump Administration cover up makes my blood boil; watching the GOP not only endorse but actively promote the rise of Authoritarianism fills me with dread.

But my anger and dread and disapproval are misplaced if I cradle them within the belief that these people who act against my interests are doing so out of some innate insidiousness and evil, to which I am immune; to buy into that self-delusion is to be as empty-headed in my assessment of them as my conservative friends are when they talk about "Lefties." I am perpetuating our mutual brokenness when I echo their disdain.

The objective, scientific truth of it all is that some people are naturally more empathetic than others; some people are more at ease in submission to the strength of a social alpha than others; some people are naturally creative, some people are naturally risk-averse. Some people prefer to act from consensus; some believe there is safety in social continuity. And *all* of these traits are inborn, often reinforced in childhood - the genetic roll of the dice, accidents of geography.

For the pious pedestrians of the Right to judge those of the Left for possessing social traits and perspectives they do not (cannot) share is the Mt. Everest of disingenuousness, yes - but it is *equally* disingenuous for those on the Left to turn around and sit in judgment of their siblings on the Right for exactly the same reasons.

It's easy to be angry. It's easy to hate, to condescend, to point fingers. It's easy to focus on the Authoritarianism and the horrific policies and the lack of understanding and conclude that the people-not-like-us are truly both stupid and morally onerous - until we realize that their social and intellectual failings, whatever they might objectively be, are the result of cognitive clustering –*exactly the same* cognitive clustering that we've been subjected to from childhood. Our tribe is as broken as theirs, for exactly the same reason - just broken in different ways: minds deprived of cognitive diversity lose their social sensitivity and awareness.

Let's call it *paleomorality*, and let's define it this way: all of us are broken. All human beings suffer from distorted worldviews, erroneous perceptions of self and others, framed by a very unnatural social universe that deprives us of an authentic, realistic sense of who we are - and fueled by the cognitive cluster, an infection that corrupts us all.

The liberal-progressives lay claim to being the truly compassionate ones, the best expression of universal human values. Okay, then, let's really be that - by extending our compassion even to those we have lately taken to despising, by recognizing our own cognitive frailty - and by truly living our values, even in the face of rising threat - even when it's the hardest thing we've ever done.

Social Dominance, Homo sapiens Style

Much has been written about, and much study has been done of social dominance. It is a phenomenon we have all seen in our study of history, if not first-hand, and we understand what it is, even if it is fairly rare.

A social dominator is a self-perceived alpha, a person whose sense of self-importance and hierarchical superiority is the driving force in their social behaviors and decisions. Not merely bossy or pushy, an SD must influence social situations in such a way as to come out on top, regardless of the cost of the effort. Any other outcome is unacceptable.

Several behavioral characteristics and cognitive features distinguish the social dominator:

- Sincere belief, justified or not, in their own superiority;
- An almost total lack of empathy;
- A absolute sense of privilege (rules aren't meant for them);
- A lack of any consistent moral code;
- An inability to admit error, or to apologize;
- A strong tendency to escalate any conflict, no matter how trivial, until they emerge victorious.

We reserve words like *cold-blooded* and *ruthless* for social dominators. They have no attachment to the truth, to fairness, to justice (except for themselves) and will say anything, in the moment, to win. They crave adoration and loyalty from others but never offer either. They are intolerant of challenge and contradiction, and will not hesitate to shame or discredit any critic by any means.

Sound like anyone you know?

A social dominator is distinct from an authoritarian leader (though it is possible to be both at once – what Robert Altemeyer calls a "double high") in several important ways. An authoritarian leader, though strictly hierarchical in social behaviors and lacking in empathy for outsiders, may still possess a moral code and an ability to negotiate – or, at least, to put limits on the escalation of aggression. Bush II and Reagan are examples of authoritarian leaders who were not social dominators.

We also see social dominance as a group dynamic, in the world around us and in history, ethnic or ideological bands of humans who collectively adopt the self-image and behaviors of a socially dominant individual in their treatment of members of another group. This sort of group dominance is generally abstract, built upon an SD leader's framing of the group to be dominated, and presents a couple of conundrums:

1. The members of the socially dominant group are not themselves social dominators; in the first place, there aren't enough SDs among us, percentage-wise, to muster such a group – and if there were, they would spend all of their time trying to dominate each other;
2. Group social dominance serves no concrete purpose in the real world - among other primates (chimpanzees), tribal combat is territorial, but there is no prehistoric evidence that humans ever indulged in it, and they wouldn't have needed to…the response to the appearance of a new and stronger group, in a world of nomads, is to simply move on.

Group social dominance in the modern world, then, generally means a social dominator leading a group of authoritarian followers to oppress another group, for concocted reasons that mobilize the followers to achieve the dominator's purposes.

Indeed, this is the *only* recipe for group social dominance: only a social dominator provides the template for such inhuman behavior, and only authoritarian followers are cognitively predisposed to outsource their social decision-making to a group leader. No other groups or cognitive types could realistically generate such outcomes.

It's not readily conceivable, then, that group social dominance occurred in prehistory. Human groups, suppressed in size by Dunbar's Number, could not have been large enough for an SD to muster a sufficient sub-group to overwhelm the entire tribe (the authoritarian predisposition, a consequence of brain component size ratios, is not genetically dominant).

Institutional social dominance, then, is a modern human innovation – probably less than 10,000 years old. It only became possible with the emergence of the first city-states. With religion as its carrier wave, however, it lost no time growing into a standard social form.

We can agree, I think, that social dominators are toxic – and that social dominance as a group dynamic is even more so: anything that causes people who are not SDs to behave like SDs is something we should guard against.

This explains how tens of millions of people who hold their moral code as precious can uplift a social dominator who possesses no moral code at all; why the dominator can deceive with impunity, label outsiders as enemies arbitrarily and not be questioned, and how otherwise good people can accept the marginalizing of their neighbors on the basis of completely fabricated threats.

The physicist Steven Weinberg had this to say: "With or without religion, good people can behave well and bad people can do evil; but for good people to do evil - that takes religion." Let's amend him a bit (acknowledging that religion is the SD standard) and say that for good people to do evil takes group social dominance – and agree to keep SDs in check.

Authoritarian followers are always scanning for a leader to protect them. Step One in preventing the group dominance dynamic from emerging is to promote a general atmosphere of safety and mutual understanding, so they won't be so quick to board the SD train. Step Two is spotting SDs as they emerge, and consigning them to television, where they belong...

"It matters not who you love, where you love, why you love, when you love or how you love – it matters only that you love."

~John Lennon

5:2

Recent events around the world are following a pattern: as globalization proceeds, economies intertwine, human mobility spikes and planetary communication settles into real-time, Authoritarianism is overtly grasping for control.

We see it in Russia. We see it in North Korea. We see it in Brexit. It's happened, unthinkably, here at home.

But yesterday, in France, Authoritarianism was put down.

And some telling numbers emerged, numbers we need to pay close attention to. The most telling was the ratio of centrist supporters to nationalism supporters – 65.8% to 34.2% (just under 2:1).

That's roughly the ratio of non-Authoritarians to Authoritarians in the general world population (5:2). Per George Lakoff, whose term for Authoritarianism is *Strict Father Morality*[9], the number is slightly less than 1/3; per Robert Altemeyer, who calls Authoritarians *High-RWAs*[10], the number is slightly more than 1/4.

Allowing for those who didn't vote, we can generalize that in France, almost all of the Authoritarians - generally rural nationalists - turned out to vote; and most, but not all, of the non-Authoritarians, likewise turned out, though not as diligently. The Authoritarians appeared in slightly higher proportion to their actual numbers, due to lower turnout among non-Authoritarians, but not much. In the end, the ratio was very nearly 2:1 - close to the distribution found in the general population.

In the US, it was a very different story. Less than half of those eligible to vote in 2016 did so; but nearly all of the Authoritarians turned out. That dropped the ratio from the general population distribution - 5:2 - to very nearly 1:1. Hillary Clinton won the popular vote by 2.3%, but as we all

---

[9] See Page 113

[10] See page 187

know, the numbers were close enough to make possible the Electoral College victory of Donald Trump.

Many reasons for this outcome have been advanced, but in the end, the numbers are what they are: Authoritarianism won in the US, and keeps winning, because Authoritarian followers are represented at the polls beyond the proportion of their numbers in the population.

Put another way, the *only* time Authoritarians can take power in a democracy, via free election, is when non-Authoritarians fail to vote. That 5:2 population ratio, which holds true everywhere, is based on a gene distribution: the predisposition toward Authoritarian cognition and behavior is genetic, and its expression will tend to conform to that ratio wherever one goes.

Authoritarians, never more than 1/3 of any population, can only take power when non-Authoritarians are too complacent to prevent it.

The message is simple: *vote*. But the implication is exhilarating: by recognizing what these numbers tell us, and acting accordingly, we can keep Authoritarianism in check, wherever democracy prevails. All we require is the will to do so.

(Turn to Page 180)

Non-Verbal

One important aspect of understanding the social behaviors and cooperative success of Paleolithic humanity is the fact that we had mastered communication with one another hundreds of thousands of years before we invented actual language. Every human was expert in non-verbal communication.

We've lost that, and worse, we pummel ourselves with remote, impersonal, digital communication day in and day out. Our reliance upon symbolic encoding of thoughts has stunted our ability to look at another person and understand their emotional state and whatever it is they are wanting to convey to us.

This is something we can each work on, in order to restore the fullness of our human legacy: we can reconnect to those abilities, work our emotional muscles and begin re-learning non-verbal communication. Couples do it to some degree, and parents can do it with their children, but past that point our people-reading skills drop off rapidly.

But it doesn't have to be this way. There is little cost and much reward in personally committing to invest in really paying attention to the faces, eyes, vocal tones and other expressions of others. It increases our understanding of them, strengthens our connections, and awakens that part of our social brains which most enjoys other people.

(Turn to Page 86)

Chuck and Roger

I recently had the pleasure of phone chats with two young Cro-Magnons in the early Upper Paleolithic, male members of a clan roaming Western Eurasia. They had lots to share about their careers, their tribe, and life as it used to be…

CHUCK

So, tell us a little about yourself. What do you do for the tribe?

I'M A SHIFT LEADER ON THE HUNTER-GATHERER TEAM.

So you go out into the savannah and…

TRACK DINNER AND FIND SIDE DISHES. MY TEAM LOVES A GOOD MAMMOTH AMBUSH. APART FROM THAT, WILD BOAR. THE OCCASIONAL REINDEER. I SOMETIMES PINCH-HIT WITH THE ROOTS-AND-BERRIES GANG.

That sounds a little dangerous. Do you consider your job risky?

FUCK, YES! POKE A 9-TON LEATHER BAG OF MUSCLE WITH A SHARP STICK ENOUGH TIMES AND HE GETS PISSED. FIVE OF MY HOMIES GOT STOMPED INTO ROADKILL IN THE PAST YEAR ALONE.

What drew you to this line of work?

SEE, IT'S IN THE DETAILS. WHEN I WAS A KID I WAS ALWAYS GOOD WITH PATTERN-FINDING GAMES – "SPOT THE HYENA," "WHERE DID LITTLE BROTHER POOP," THAT SORT OF THING. HAVING THAT KNACK COMES IN HANDY WHEN EVERYONE'S FEELING PECKISH AND IT'S RAINING LIKE HELL AND YOU HAVE TO FIGURE OUT WHERE ALL THE CARIBOU WENT.

What do you like best about it?

WELL, THE SCENERY CHANGES, YOU KNOW? AND MARCHING BACK INTO CAMP WITH LOTS OF GOODIES INSPIRES... OH, LET'S SAY, 'GRATITUDE' AMONG SOME OF OUR CURVIER CITIZENS.

Is there a downside to hunting and gathering?

WELL, THE AFOREMENTIONED GETTING-TRAMPLED THING IS ALWAYS A CONCERN, BUT ALMOST AS BAD IS THE PROSPECT OF GETTING LOST AND NEVER RECONNECTING WITH THE CLAN. I MEAN, THIS ISN'T AN ENVIRONMENT THAT'S PARTICULARLY CONDUCIVE TO AUTONOMY.

Is there anything you'd rather be doing?

SOMETIMES I FIND MYSELF HUMMING A CATCHY TUNE, AND I WONDER IF I PULL OFF A SET OR TWO AT CAMPFIRE.

How would others in the tribe describe you?

I THINK YOU'D FIND I'M WELL-LIKED AMONG THE CLAN IN GENERAL. I'M QUICK WITH A HIGH-FIVE OR A ONE-LINER. SOMETIMES I GO TOO FAR, I SUPPOSE. GOOSING TRIBAL ELDERS. PANTSING THE FIRE-TENDER.

What are your political views?

MY FRIENDS WOULD TELL YOU I'M A PROGRESSIVE LIBERAL, AND I CERTAINLY THINK THAT'S FAIR... BUT I'M LESS SANGUINE ABOUT RESOURCE ALLOCATION THEORY THAN MY PEERS. IT'S LESS A QUESTION OF OPTIMIZATION FOR THE SAKE OF EQUILIBRIUM, AND MORE A QUESTION OF HOW FAST A ROTTING MAMMOTH WILL DRAW A CROWD IF YOU DON'T STRIP IT AND EAT IT IN A HURRY.

What does 'progressive' entail, in your world?

WELL, IT'S ALL ABOUT EATING, ISN'T IT? ICE AGE OR NO, THE WORLD IS FUCKING BURSTING WITH FOOD – YOU JUST NEED TO GET OUT THERE AND GO AFTER IT. SO, WHEN I THINK 'PROGRESSIVE,' I THINK, 'ASS IN GEAR'...

Would you describe your tribe as a society?

IT'S EASY TO BE CRITICAL, YOU KNOW? WE LACK THE OBVIOUS ADVANTAGES OF HOMICIDAL RAGE WE OBSERVE IN OUR SIMIAN COUSINS. AND SOME OTHER SPECIES WATCHING US MIGHT JUDGE, AND SAY WE HAVE WAYYYY TOO MUCH SEX.

BUT IT'S ALWAYS BEEN MY FEELING THAT DESPITE OUR OBVIOUS PHYSICAL DISADVANTAGES, AS A SPECIES WE KICK SOME SERIOUS ASS.

ROGER

So, tell us a little about yourself. What do you do for the tribe?

THIS.

This, meaning…?

THIS. SITTING HERE, I MEAN. BY THE FIRE. IT IS MY JOB TO TEND THE FIRE. KEEP IT GOING THRU THE NIGHT.

To stay warm.

TO STAY NOT DEAD. THE FIRE KEEPS FELIX AWAY.

Felix…

BIG CATS. THE ONES THAT EAT US. WE CALL THEM FELIX. FELIXES. FELIX CAN SEE IN THE DARK, AND WE, YOU KNOW, CAN'T, BUT FELIX IS SCARED OF FIRE. SO MY JOB IS TO KEEP FELIX AWAY AT NIGHT.

How long have you been doing this job?

ABOUT AN HOUR AND A HALF.

No, I mean, altogether. As a career.

OH. SORRY. SINCE I WAS... AH... LET'S SEE... THREE YEARS OLD. NO, FOUR. NO, THREE. THREE.

What drew you to this line of work?

WANTING TO NOT GET EATEN.

What do you like best about it?

WELL, IT'S EASY ON THE BACK AND ON THE MIND, AND THE BENEFITS ARE GOOD. BUT THE HOURS TOTALLY SUCK.

Is there a downside to keeping Felix away?

SEE, THE THING IS, YOU KNOW HE'S OUT THERE, SO YOU'RE ALWAYS KIND OF AWARE OF HIM. SO I'M ALWAYS SCANNING FOR HIM, ALWAYS A LITTLE BIT AFRAID.

Is there anything you'd rather be doing?

I THINK I'D DO WELL IN THE FINANCIAL SECTOR.

How would others in the tribe describe you?

THAT'S NOT AN EASY QUESTION. YOU HAVE TO UNDERSTAND THAT WE DON'T HAVE THE NUMBERS TO EFFECTIVELY SEGREGATE, THOUGH I CAN SEE AN UPSIDE. SOME OF THE YOUNG PEOPLE ARE BELLIGERENT, UNCOUTH. ONE OF THEM KEEPS PANTSING ME.

What are your political views?

I LIKE TO THINK OF MYSELF AS SOCIALLY LIBERAL, BUT FISCALLY CONSERVATIVE.

What does 'conservative' entail, in your world?

WELL, IT'S ALL ABOUT SURVIVAL, ISN'T IT? THE WORLD IS SCARY AS SHIT, AND NOT EVERYONE AROUND HERE HAS ENOUGH

COMMON SENSE TO SEE THAT. SO WHEN I THINK 'CONSERVATIVE,' I THINK 'PEOPLE WHO PREFER TO NOT GET EATEN.'

Would you describe your tribe as a society?

WELL, WE HAVE WAYYYYYY TOO MUCH SEX, IF YOU ASK ME. SOME OF OUR FEMALES ARE... IMMODEST AT TIMES. IT MAKES ME REALLY UNCOMFORTABLE. AND FREQUENTLY SELF-CONSCIOUS. LESS OF THAT, I THINK, AND MORE OF THE HOMICIDAL RAGE OF OUR SIMIAN COUSINS, AND I THINK WE'D SOMEDAY RULE THE WORLD...

(Turn to Page 101)

Nuclear Family Holocaust

Human community is broken, and we are born into a world that very much works against the natural function of our social brains.

Almost all of our social institutions, arrangements and defaults are non-optimal for our social brains - in particular, the most recent innovation, the nuclear family.

"Mom, Dad and the kids" was utterly impossible during the Paleolithic. In the first place, we weren't monogamous; in the second, we weren't too fussy about who dad was; in the third, we all shared the same living space - suburbs hadn't been invented. "Family" meant half a dozen associated sub-groups temporarily occupying several square miles, including a hundred or so people - all of whom we knew as well as today's nuclear family members know each other (or better).

Paternity was not a question for many reasons: we have no idea when it dawned on our genus that sex and birth, being separated by 9 months, were causally connected (no one needs that knowledge for the system to work); every female had several favored males of her own selection, and it is very probable that she would enjoy them one after the other, when she was in the mood; there was no wealth or property to pass down to one's progeny, even if you know who they were; entire tribes raised the young together (it takes a village).

This arrangement worked optimally for humanity for hundreds of thousands of years - until property was invented, and it became possible for one man to have power over many, and for all men to have power over all women.

What does this have to do with the nuclear family?

The social frame of the nuclear family places a tremendous strain on the couple making the attempt. It is no wonder at all that the failure rate has skyrocketed as the church's hold on society has weakened, and as social pressure has yielded to diversity. A man and a woman attempting to get thru the challenges of creating a family and dealing with the surrounding society and its economics are increasingly disadvantaged.

Within society's strict rules for coupling, monogamy being only the most obvious, a man and a woman must meet a tremendous range of needs in one another, most of them transcending sex. To succeed, they must cultivate a staggering array of functional intimacies, filling multiple roles in one another's lives, and they must do it in explicit denial of the emotional and intimate support from outside their partnership that they would have enjoyed in prehistory. In short, they must be all things to one another, and they must muster the energy to do so without drawing energy from beyond themselves. Oh, there's usually a best friend or a supportive sibling to turn to, but that's a drop in the bucket.

In the distant past, these boundaries could not have existed. Emotional support emanated from all sides. The level of mutual understanding required for group survival enabled high transparency and intricate communication, and there were few social distinctions to diminish the depth of that transparency and communication. We were very close to the others in our tribes, depended upon one another deeply, and each filled multiple roles for others.

And if being a couple today is tough, being a parent is far tougher. Children in the Paleolithic had it great: they were never apart from the adults in the group; many if not most of those adults knew each child and could offer care and support; the children were never sequestered away from the group for any purpose but safety, and even then they were well-attended. No child ever lacked for affection and support - each enjoyed an abundance.

Cro-Magnon children were not boxed into rooms together for half of every day with a lone adult, floundering in their own lack of social knowledge and experience while siphoning dribbles of it from the adult; they were immersed in the day-to-day knowledge and activity of all adults, all the time - their schoolhouse was the world. They were not nurseried away when adults needed to confer; they were sitting right there among them.

The modern parent must provide all of this knowledge, protection and support for their children single-handedly, save tribal education - and for that, a single adult is plugged into the role, and explicitly forbidden to offer any non-academic support: teachers are forced to be anti-parents, which only increases the parent's burden. Of course, each family has a few surrogates with whom they trust their children's safety - a few family members or close neighbors - but, again, this is a drop in the bucket.

And that's before we even get to the cognitive diversity problem. A modern couple must choose a cognitively similar (if not identical) partner, for a number of reasons: first, our society does not celebrate or teach cognitive diversity, so we are not trained to be comfortable with it; second, our conflict resolution skills are minimal, compared to our Cro-Magnon parents (or even, for that matter, contemporary bonobos, who are far more cooperative than we), and so we need to live with someone who will usually agree with us; third, our coupled lives are sufficiently insular that our pooled problem-solving skills, for which cognitive diversity exists, are insufficient in any case - we are protected from the problems that threaten our lives, and usually incompetent to jointly solve the ones that don't.

But the cognitive diversity problem only gets worse with insulated reproduction. If we marry someone of our own cognitive type, the majority of our offspring will likely share that type, resulting in a family where most think in the same limited ways. This is terrible for the offspring, because they develop little awareness of cognitive variety (especially if the family associates with same-type families), and worst of all for the child or two who do *not* inherit their parents' cognitive type: they are doomed to feel like outsiders in their own homes - black sheep, not as accepted as the others, somehow different and therefore less.

Put it all together, and the deck is very much stacked against the modern nuclear family. A domestic couple is expected to achieve far too much with far too little, to enter into the most important roles human beings fill for one another while crippled from the start - and all of this deficit cripples, in turn, the children in the house.

What Are People For?

Our economic systems are built on market thinking, the juggling of resources in response to demand, with human labor as the meter.

But we have the technology now to gradually eliminate labor (and, in many cases already, not so gradually), and to throttle resources far more efficiently. In short, we have the foundation of technology that can eliminate the need for markets within two generations, probably less, if we develop the political will to do so.

The problem: human beings (not all, but many) judge other human beings by their productivity potential *vis-a-vis* the market. And this judgment is as old as human writing, as entrenched as our most prevalent religions.

Put another way, we can enter a new phase of human progress - but don't think enough of ourselves to proceed with it.

What do we do about that?

"I have seen much to criticize in mankind. But I believe there's even more to admire."

~Questor

Recommended Reading

The Age of Empathy: Nature's Lessons for a Kinder Society, Frans de Waal. Crown, 2009.

The Authoritarian Specter, Robert Altemeyer.Harvard University Press, 1996.

The Authoritarians, Robert Altemeyer.Internet e-book, 2006.

The Creation of Inequality, Kent Flannery, Joyce Marcus.Harvard University Press, 2012.

I Am a Strange Loop, Douglas Hofstadter. Basic Books, 2007.

The Meaning of Human Existence, Edward O. Wilson.Liveright, 2015.

The Moral Animal: Why We Are the Way We Are, Robert Wright. Vintage Books, 1994.

The Moral Molecule: The New Science of What Makes Us Good and Evil, Paul Zak. Corgi Books, 2013.

Moral Politics: How Liberals and Conservatives Think, George Lakoff. University of Chicago Press, 1996, 2002.

The Neuroscience of Human Relationships, Louis Cozolino. W.W. Norton, 2014.

Non-Zero: The Logic of Human Destiny, Robert Wright. Vintage, 2000.

Political Animals: How Our Stone-Age Brain Gets in the Way of Smart Politics, Rick Shenkman. Basic Books, 2016.

Our Political Nature: The Evolutionary Origins of What Divides Us, AviTuschman. Prometheus Books, 2013.

The Political Mind: A Cognitive Scientist's Guide to Your Brain and Its Politics, George Lakoff. Penguin Books, 2008.

Predisposed: Liberals, Conservatives, and the Biology of Political Differences, John R. Hibbing, Kevin B. Smith, John A. Alford. Routledge, 2014.

Prehistory: The Making of the Human Mind, Colin Renfrew. Modern Library, 2007.

The Righteous Mind: Why Good People Are Divided by Politics and Religion, Jonathan Haidt. Vintage, 2013.

Sapiens, Yuval Noah Harari.Vintage, 2011.

Seducing Ourselves: Understanding Public Denial in a Declining Complex Society, Donna Armstrong. CreateSpace, 2014.

Social: Why Our Brains Are Wired to Connect, Matthew D. Leiberman. Broadway Books, 2013.

Synaptic Self: How Our Brains Become Who We Are, Joseph LeDoux. Viking, 2002.

The Tangled Wing: Biological Constraints on the Human Spirit, Melvin Konner. Owl Books, 2003.

The World Until Yesterday, Jared Diamond.Penguin, 2012.

Why I Left, Why I Stayed: Conversations on Christianity Between an Evangelical Father and His Humanist Son, Tony Campolo, Bart Campolo. HarperOne, 2017.

About the Author

Scott Robinson is a journalist, social scientist, public speaker and musician, and was for 20 years a music critic with the *Louisville Courier-Journal*. He has also been published in *Rolling Stone* and *The Wall Street Journal*. He can be found at**www.facebook.com/scottrobinson99**.

www.ingramcontent.com/pod-product-compliance
Lightning Source LLC
Chambersburg PA
CBHW081342280526
45787CB00011B/2360